SURVIVAL
FOR BEGINNERS

SURVIVAL
FOR BEGINNERS

A STEP-BY-STEP GUIDE TO CAMPING AND OUTDOOR SKILLS

WRITTEN BY
COLIN TOWELL

Senior Editor Carron Brown
Senior Designer Sheila Collins
Designer Kit Lane
Editors Ann Baggaley, Jessica Cawthra,
Sarah Edwards, Anna Streiffert Limerick,
Georgina Palffy, Alison Sturgeon, Hannah Wilson
Designers Chrissy Barnard, Rachael Grady
Illustrations Dynamo Ltd, SJC – Stuart Jackson Carter,
Good Illustration, KJA, Gus Scott
Managing Editor Francesca Baines
Managing Art Editor Philip Letsu
Producer, Pre-Production Andy Hilliard
Producer Jude Crozier
Jacket Editor Emma Dawson
Jacket Designer Suhita Dharamjit
Senior DTP Designer Harish Aggarwal
Jackets Editorial Coordinator Priyanka Sharma
Managing Jackets Editor Saloni Singh
Jacket Design Development Manager Sophia MTT
Publisher Andrew Macintyre
Art Director Karen Self
Associate Publishing Director Liz Wheeler
Design Director Phil Ormerod
Publishing Director Jonathan Metcalf

First published in Great Britain in 2019 by
Dorling Kindersley Limited
80 Strand, London, WC2R 0RL

A Penguin Random House Company
Copyright © 2019 Dorling Kindersley Limited
2 4 6 8 10 9 7 5 3 1
001–310146–May/2019

A CIP catalogue record for this book
is available from the British Library.

Disclaimer: Whilst the publisher has taken all reasonable
care that the advice given in this book is correct, it is not
engaged in providing specific advice to individual
readers. The publisher can therefore not accept any
liability for any loss or injury sustained by anyone
following the advice in this book.
ISBN: 978-0-2413-3989-3
Printed and bound in China

A WORLD OF IDEAS:
SEE ALL THERE IS TO KNOW

www.dk.com

CONTENTS

▶ NAVIGATION 12

HOW TO USE THIS BOOK

This book is packed with outdoor activities, some simple while others are potentially hazardous.

Please always bear in mind:

• Don't deliberately put yourself in harm's way to try out the more hazardous activities, such as escape a crocodile or deal with a shark.

• Always carry out the more hazardous activities under adult supervision. Those activities have been marked with this symbol.

• Use your common sense, and do proper research and initial practice before attempting the activities for real.

• Bear in mind that any medical conditions may make activities more difficult or your condition worse – consult your doctor first.

• Take care and be responsible with every activity, not just the ones marked as hazardous, to ensure you are safe.

FOREWORD
▶▶▶ **BY COLIN TOWELL**

I am often asked what is the most terrifying survival situation
I have been in, but, although I have operated in some of the
world's most hostile environments, I have never actually found
myself in a true "life or death" survival situation. Am I just lucky?
Maybe, but as they say in the military, "luck favours those
who are best prepared".

While some survival situations do happen through sheer
bad luck, most arise from a sequence of events that could have
been avoided. When sitting on top of a mountain suffering from
hypothermia, it is too late to realize that you should have either
checked the weather forecast and packed warm clothing
before you set out, or turned back when the weather
looked like changing!

Hiking, camping, and exploring the outdoors are great fun and
hugely rewarding, but remember the wise old survival saying:
"knowledge weighs nothing and takes up no room in your pack".
With this book, you will learn essential outdoor craft and survival
techniques that will help you avoid survival situations and
show you what to do if the unfortunate does happen.

PREPARE YOURSELF

There is a wide range of high-tech outdoor gear, but the **most important kit** is the most **simple**, along with your **skills** and **will to survive**. You may need to rely on these should the high-tech fail! The key factor for a successful wilderness adventure is **preparation**. Make your **priorities protection**, **location**, **water**, and **food**.

TIP

Understand your limits and don't attempt to go beyond what you or your gear are fit to cope with.

PROTECTION

Protect yourself against the elements and injury:

- Prepare for changing weather conditions, such as a cold snap, and plan your kit accordingly.

- A positive attitude, together with knowledge and experience, will help you make good decisions.

- Set realistic and achievable goals.

- Don't go on an adventure to get fit – get fit to go on an adventure by stepping up your exercise routine.

LOCATION

Survival and rescue can depend on location. When you plan your trip, ask yourself:

- Is the area I am going to dangerous?

- Will people know where to look for me?

- Will I be able to attract their attention?

WATER

Water is life. No one can survive for more than a few days without it.

- Carry sufficient water (always more than you think).

- Have the means to filter and disinfect untreated water.

- Plan your route around water sources.

- Remember, if you are in a hot country, are unwell, or injured, having enough water will be even more important.

FOOD

In a short-term survival situation, food will not be too important, but you must eat to stay fit and healthy.

- Start your adventure with a good meal – it's like filling up a fuel tank.

- Pack snacks and trail mix that are easy to ration out over a few days.

- Plan your food rations carefully – allow for unscheduled days on the trail.

KIT LAYERS

The **gear** you carry should be grouped into **three categories**: first-line, second-line, and third-line kit. This equipment ranges from items that would be **essential** to your survival – first-line kit – to equipment that may be regarded as luxuries. If the worst happens, what you have in your daypack or pockets could be all you have to rely on.

Re-assess where your kit is stowed as conditions change throughout the day.

FIRST-LINE KIT

This is basic survival gear to keep with you at all times: worn as clothing, clipped to a belt, or stowed in a pocket.

- Suitable clothing (including waterproofs), plus hat, gloves, and sunglasses
- Map (in waterproof cover), compass, GPS unit
- Mobile phone and spare power pack
- Watch
- Water bottle, with filtration/disinfection system
- Headtorch and spare batteries
- Pocketknife with small saw blade
- Safety whistle
- Survival tin (see pages 10–11)
- Firelighting kit (lighter/flint and steel/matches/cotton wool balls)
- Tissues/toilet paper

SECOND-LINE KIT

Gear to keep you safe for a whole day out, this is kit you carry from your base camp in a small daypack.

- Spare set of clothes, including socks, hat, and gloves
- Bothy bag (see page 89)
- Rations for the day (+1 day extra)
- First aid kit
- Metal cup (for boiling water)
- Camping stove
- Extra water

For quick access, keep essentials in a secure pocket.

THIRD-LINE KIT

Survival equipment to keep you going for longer than just one night, third-line kit is carried in a larger backpack.

- Shelter: tent, tarp, or shelter sheet
- Sleeping system: sleeping bag and sleeping mat
- Cooking equipment: stove and cooking pots
- Wash kit and sanitary items
- Extra water
- Dry bag liner for backpack

If you prioritize your kit, you can be sure of having all essential items to hand whenever you need them.

A **basic survival tin** should be **compact** enough for you to **carry at all times** and contain **useful items** that will address the immediate **priorities of survival**: protection, location, and water. Your tin is always a "work in progress" and can be adapted to suit your environment and your needs.

AFTER AN ADVENTURE, REPLACE ITEMS IN YOUR TIN IF YOU USED THEM.

CHOOSING A TIN

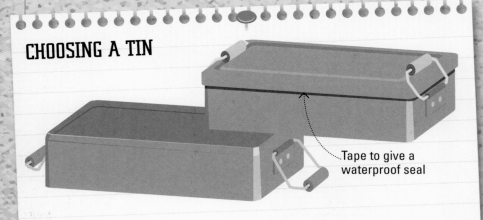

Tape to give a waterproof seal

Metal
A survival tin can be any size but should be metal so you can use it to boil water in if needed.

Waterproof
To keep contents dry, use a waterproof tin or seal the lid to the container with electrical tape.

The inside of the lid can be polished and used as a signal mirror (see page 37).
Additional items can be taped to the inside of the lid, such as: a sailmaker's needle, safety pins, and mini glow sticks.

PACKING THE TIN

Packing a tin is an art. Choose items carefully and add those relevant to your environment and needs. Go for quality not quantity – your life may depend on it.

A selection of items form several layers of the tin. See opposite for which items go in which layer.

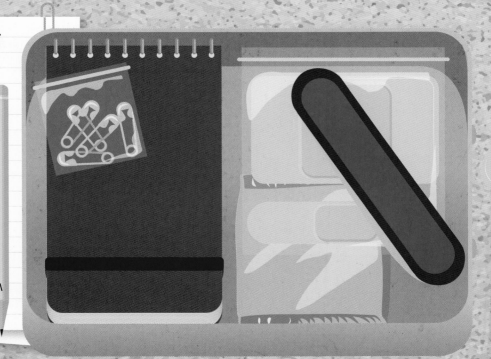

THE LAYERS OF THE TIN

Choose items that are "fit for purpose" and learn how to use them.

Layer 1
Minor first aid items and water purification

Layer 2
Medical and the ability to leave notes

- First aid items, such as waterproof plasters and adhesive suture strips
- Medical wipes
- Water purification tablets

Layer 1 (bottom layer)

- Ziplock bag of petroleum jelly
- Waterproof notepaper
- Local paper money
- Pencil or waterproof pen

Layer 2

Layer 3
Quality essential items that have specific uses for survival

Layer 4
Firelighting and additional items that you figure out you need through experience

- Needle already threaded with strong cotton
- Small photon keyring torch
- Small pocketknife
- Compact compass or quality button compass

Layer 3

- Flint and steel
- Mini fishing kit with strong line
- Safety pins

Layer 4

ADDITIONAL KIT

Choose additional items that you are able to carry, and which are relevant to your needs. Here are some ideas for compact and light extra items that can be useful.

Plastic bags
Bin bags can be used to keep items dry or to carry water.

Small candle
Once lit, a candle provides a reliable flame to help light your fire.

Tights
Nylon tights take up no weight or room but can be used for warmth, as a mosquito net, or improvised fishing net.

Space/survival blanket
This thin, silver, waterproof sheet can be used as a shelter (see pages 88–89) or for an emergency signal (see page 37).

NAVIGATION

GETTING LOST AND UNDERESTIMATING THE TERRAIN ARE TWO OF THE MOST COMMON REASONS WHY PEOPLE FIND THEMSELVES IN TROUBLE. A BASIC UNDERSTANDING OF HOW TO USE A MAP AND COMPASS IS KEY.

Keeping on track
Planning an achievable and safe route before you set off will ensure that you have the knowledge to alter your route when necessary.

A map is a flat, **graphic representation of a 3D area**. From a map, you can determine **distance and height** on the ground. If you are able to read and interpret a map, you can **visualize the terrain** you will be walking across, identifying **map features** as **landmarks** to help you navigate.

> NAVIGATING IS ALL ABOUT TRUSTING YOUR MAP AND COMPASS.

Cairn helps to identify starting point.

STEP BY STEP

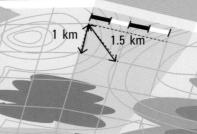

❶ Set your map (see pages 18–19). Line a pencil up between your location and a map feature. Turn the map until the pencil points to the same spot on the ground.

❷ Estimate the distance between features. On a 1:25,000 scale map, a 4 cm (1½ in) grid square represents 1 km (⅔ mile); each diagonal represents 1.5 km (1 mile).

❸ Alternatively, measure the distance with a piece of string, following curves in the route, then measure the length of string against the scale bar.

Hills, valleys, ridges, and spurs can be matched to contour lines on the map.

6 See if the shapes of features on the map are replicated on the ground. Look out for such things as curves in the path, areas of woodland, lakes, rivers, and roads.

Bends in the road can be identified on the map.

The shape and type of woodland can help establish your location.

4 Identify features on the ground, such as farm buildings and marshy areas, using the map symbols. See if they align. How close are they?

5 Match relief – the height and shape of hills, valleys, ridges, saddles, and spurs – on the ground to contour lines on the map (see pages 16–17).

Hill alongside lake

UNDERSTANDING MAPS

Topographic maps are best for hiking. These show **natural and man-made features** such as rivers and paths, and depict the lie of the land with **contour lines** to represent height. They incorporate a **legend** to decipher the information shown on the map, a **grid** to help locate specific points, and a **scale bar** to indicate distance.

SCALE

The scale is a ratio of how much you would have to enlarge the map to reach actual size. A 1:25,000 map, on which 4 cm represents 1 km (2½ in to 1 mile), is useful for hiking.

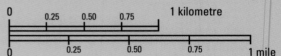

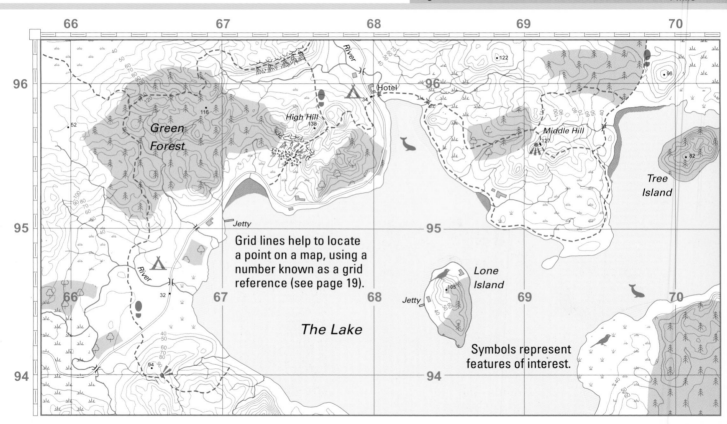

Grid lines help to locate a point on a map, using a number known as a grid reference (see page 19).

Symbols represent features of interest.

MAP LEGEND

A legend, or key, deciphers the information shown on the map. Knowing the symbols used will help you to visualize what is being represented on the map.

Natural features and height

Water	Shingle
Mud	Scree
Sand	Vertical face/cliff

Vegetation

Coniferous trees
Non-coniferous trees
Scrub
Bracken/heath
Marsh

Tourist and leisure

Fishing area
Campsite
Walks/trails
Viewpoint
Nature reserve

VISUALIZING RELIEF

Contour lines join points of **equal height above sea level**, revealing the shape of the ground in detail. The ability to imagine how **contour lines translate to the ground** will help you to read a map. Knowing how steep the ground is will **help you plan your route**.

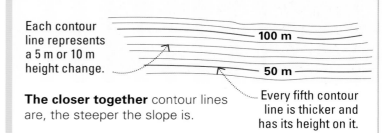

Each contour line represents a 5 m or 10 m height change.

100 m

50 m

The closer together contour lines are, the steeper the slope is.

Every fifth contour line is thicker and has its height on it.

100 m

50 m

Contour lines run all the way around a hill in a closed ring. How close the lines are will give you an idea how steep the hill is.

Parallel contour lines with high ground in the middle show a ridge. Walking up and down uses a lot of energy, so follow lines around instead.

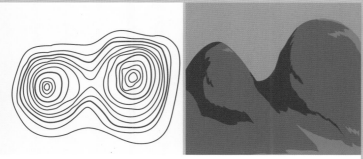

A saddle has two ring contour patterns with lower ground in between – like two hills joined by a ridge that dips in the middle.

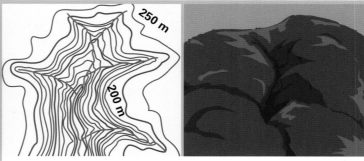

250 m

200 m

A valley is indicated by a series of hairpin bends, with the bends pointing uphill. Check the contour numbers to work out which way a valley slopes.

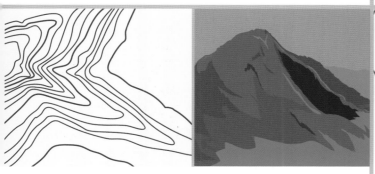

A spur, jutting out from the side of a hill, is shown by a series of hairpin bends, with the bends pointing downhill.

A valley that runs down a hillside, often between spurs, can be identified as a series of contour lines that point uphill.

USE A COMPASS

A compass has a **needle,** which is a **magnetized piece of metal**. When allowed to rotate freely, the needle will point towards **Earth's magnetic North Pole**. Use a compass to determine **direction,** orientate (line up) yourself and your map, work out **bearings,** and **navigate** from one place to another.

ALWAYS HOLD A COMPASS LEVEL AND WAIT A FEW MOMENTS FOR IT TO SETTLE. IT WILL POINT TO MAGNETIC NORTH.

MAP SYMBOLS - SEE PAGES 16-17

Orienting arrow points to compass point N

The red end of the needle always points to magnetic north. The white end points to magnetic south.

Orienting lines

Hole for attaching cord

Rotating dial

The number of degrees indicates the bearing.

STEP BY STEP

❶ First you need to "set your map". This means orienting the map to your surroundings. To do this, take your compass and rotate the dial so that the N on the dial lines up with the index line. The N on the dial should point towards the direction of travel arrow. Don't worry about what the needle is doing.

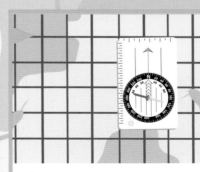

❷ Lay the map on the ground. Line up the long side of your compass with the vertical grid lines (eastings). The direction of travel arrow points to the top of the map.

❸ Keeping the compass aligned with the eastings, carefully rotate the entire map until the needle points to N on the dial. The map is now set to magnetic north.

MAGNETIC VARIATION

Magnetic variation is the difference between magnetic north on your compass and grid north on your map (see page 21). It can be either east or west or a large or small variation depending where you are in the world.

As you advance with map and compass skills, attend a class on magnetic variation in order to understand how it applies to the area you are in. A class will teach you that:

⬤ When you work out a route bearing on a map, you need to compensate for (add or subtract) the variation to your compass before setting off.
⬤ The same principle applies to transferring a bearing taken on your compass and plotting it on a map.
⬤ Over short distances, you can usually ignore the variation but for longer distances, such as over 2 km (1 mile), it should be done.

The direction of travel arrow points to the direction in which you should walk.

GRID REFERENCES

Use the grid lines on this map to describe the location of the grey square. This is a "grid reference".

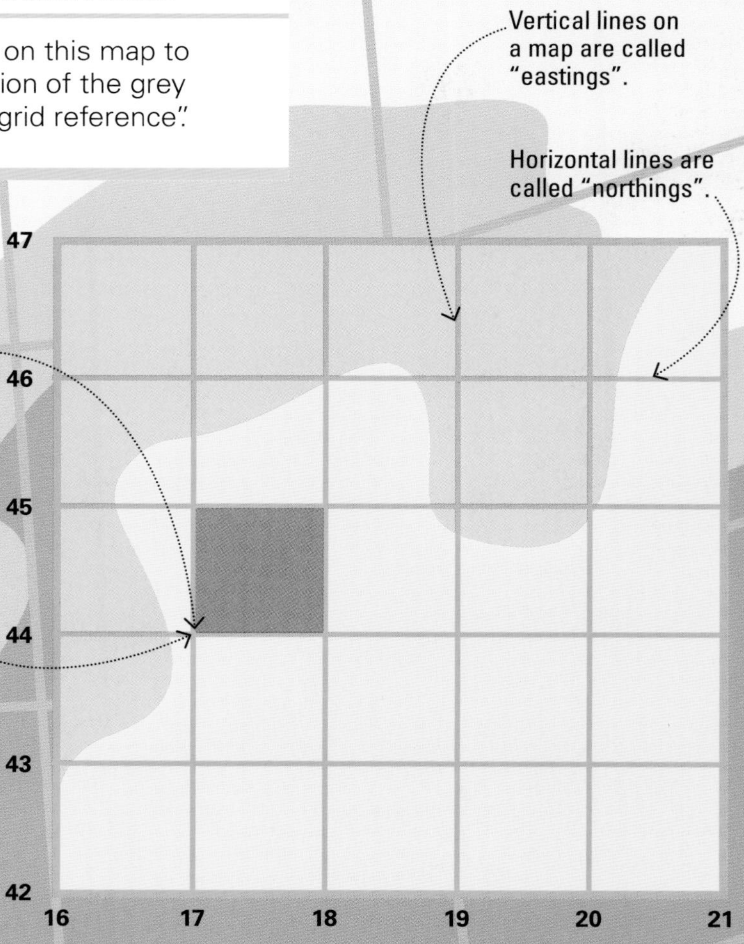

Vertical lines on a map are called "eastings".

Horizontal lines are called "northings".

The index line is an extension of the direction of travel arrow.

1 Give the number of the easting at the bottom left-hand corner of the square.

2 Then give the number of the northing in that corner.

3 The grid reference for this square is 1744.

4 You now know that the top of the map is pointing to magnetic north. Features on the map should more or less line up with those that you can see around you.

47
46
45
44
43
42

16   17   18   19   20   21

NAVIGATE WITH A COMPASS

When out hiking, you need to know where you are, so you **do not get lost.** Also, if you do have an emergency, you need to be able to let others know exactly where you are. **Use a compass and map** to work out which direction to take to reach your destination. Map reading and compass navigation are **great skills** to have. It's fun to practise them whenever you are hiking.

> **DON'T RUSH YOUR COMPASS WORK. ERRORS COULD GET YOU LOST.**

Can you see your destination? Use your eyes as well as the compass.

Trees or other features of the terrain may block the view of your destination.

Keep an eye on obvious landmarks to help you work out where you are.

STEP BY STEP

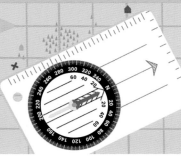

❶ Lay your map on flat, dry ground. Make sure there is nothing metal nearby, such as a zip or mobile phone. These could interfere with the magnetic compass.

❷ Lay the edge of the compass so that it runs between where you are and where you want to go. The direction of travel arrow points to your destination.

❸ Turn the compass dial until the orienting lines align with the vertical eastings on the map. The orienting arrow will point to the top of the map. Ignore the needle.

Finding **south** in the **southern hemisphere** is not quite as easy as finding north in the northern hemisphere, but it can be done. You need to locate the four main stars of the **Southern Cross constellation** and the bright stars known as the **pointers** as guides.

PRACTISE LOCATING THE POSITION OF THE STARS THROUGHOUT THE YEAR.

2 Find the two bright pointer stars that lie to the side of the constellation and join them with an imaginary line. Imagine another line extending at right angles from the centre until it crosses the line from the Southern Cross.

Southern Cross

Pointers

1 The stars of the Southern Cross form a kite shape. Draw an imaginary diagonal line through this shape and extend it downwards from the constellation.

3 The point where the two lines cross is the South Celestial Pole. Drop a vertical line to the horizon to locate approximate south.

South

THE SOUTHERN CROSS YEAR ROUND

The Southern Cross and the pointer stars rotate clockwise around the South Celestial Pole throughout the year. They hold the same positions in relation to each other, no matter how they are oriented in the sky.

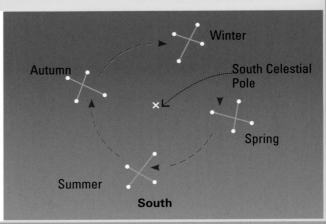

Winter

Autumn

South Celestial Pole

Spring

Summer

South

If you don't have a compass, and can't see the sun, you can **turn to nature** to get an idea of **directions**. Knowing the prevailing **wind direction**, or whether major **roads, rivers, or railways** run in particular directions, can also help you figure out where you are and where to go.

The side facing the sun has denser foliage and, depending on species and season, more buds, flowers, fruits, or nuts.

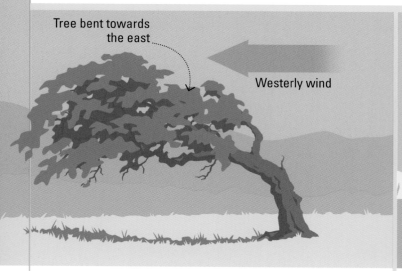

Tree bent towards the east

Westerly wind

Over the years, trees in windswept areas grow bending away from the wind. So, if the prevailing wind in an area is westerly, tree shapes will be pointing towards the east.

Tree growth is the most lush on the side that faces the sun. Remember that this means south in the Northern Hemisphere, but if you are in the Southern Hemisphere it means north.

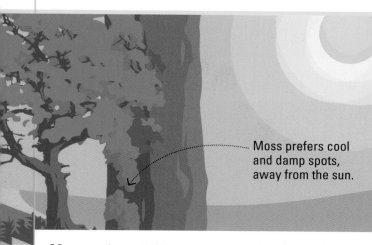

Moss prefers cool and damp spots, away from the sun.

Moss and most lichens grow on the shady sides of objects, out of direct sunlight. So, they grow on the north side in the northern hemisphere and on the south side in the Southern Hemisphere.

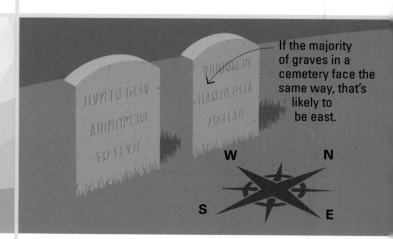

If the majority of graves in a cemetery face the same way, that's likely to be east.

W   N

S   E

In many Western cultures, gravestones traditionally face the rising sun. This practice is no longer always followed, so look for older graves, and compare with natural signs to make sure.

In very windy areas, where the wind direction is constant, birds tend to nest on the leeside of hills to be more sheltered. To read this sign correctly, you need to know the prevailing wind in the area.

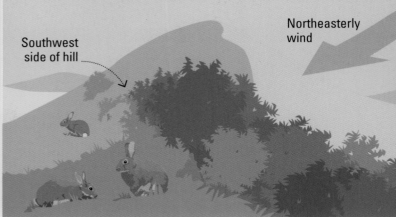

Small animals burrow on the leeside of windswept hills. If you know the prevailing wind direction, look out for rabbit holes, or other small dens, for an idea of the direction the slope faces.

Many anthills use the sun to regulate their inside temperature, and tend to face towards it to catch as much sunlight as possible. This is not always the case, so use along with other signs.

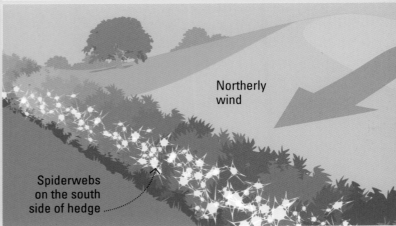

Spiders usually spin their webs in the sheltered side of trees, buildings, hedges, and fences, so the wind doesn't break or destroy their webs – so you need to know the prevailing winds.

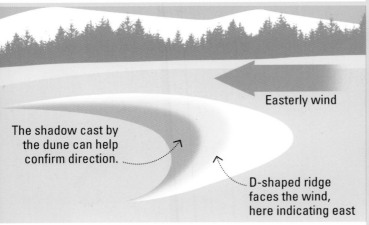

If you know the prevailing wind, observing the shape of snow dunes can help you determine direction. Prevailing winds form D-shaped dunes with the curve of the D pointing into the wind.

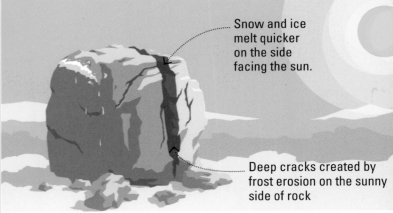

Frost erosion, happens when water repeatedly freezes and thaws on rocks and bare mountain sides. It usually creates the most severe vertical cracks on the part facing the sun.

A **Global Positioning System** (GPS) is a handheld device that uses signals from a group of **24 orbiting satellites** in space to work out exact locations on Earth. A GPS is useful for working out straight line **distances and bearings** to and from a point, but unless it incorporates **mapping**, it will not show the best way to get there. A GPS device can be used to play an outdoor treasure-hunting game known as **geocaching**.

Menus and features vary, so practise using your GPS device before you travel.

The receiver locks onto at least four satellites to obtain the exact location, displayed as a grid reference.

The screen lights up for use in gloomy conditions.

Durable, waterproof case

GEOCACHING

Use your GPS device to navigate to a specific set of GPS coordinates, then try to find a hidden geocache (container).

STEP BY STEP

❶ Register with a cache listing site. Search for caches near you and choose one that interests you. Record any notes or hints on a notepad.

❷ Create a route on your GPS device, using the coordinates on the cache listing site. Follow the arrow on the screen to navigate to the cache.

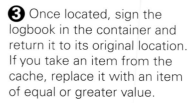

❸ Once located, sign the logbook in the container and return it to its original location. If you take an item from the cache, replace it with an item of equal or greater value.

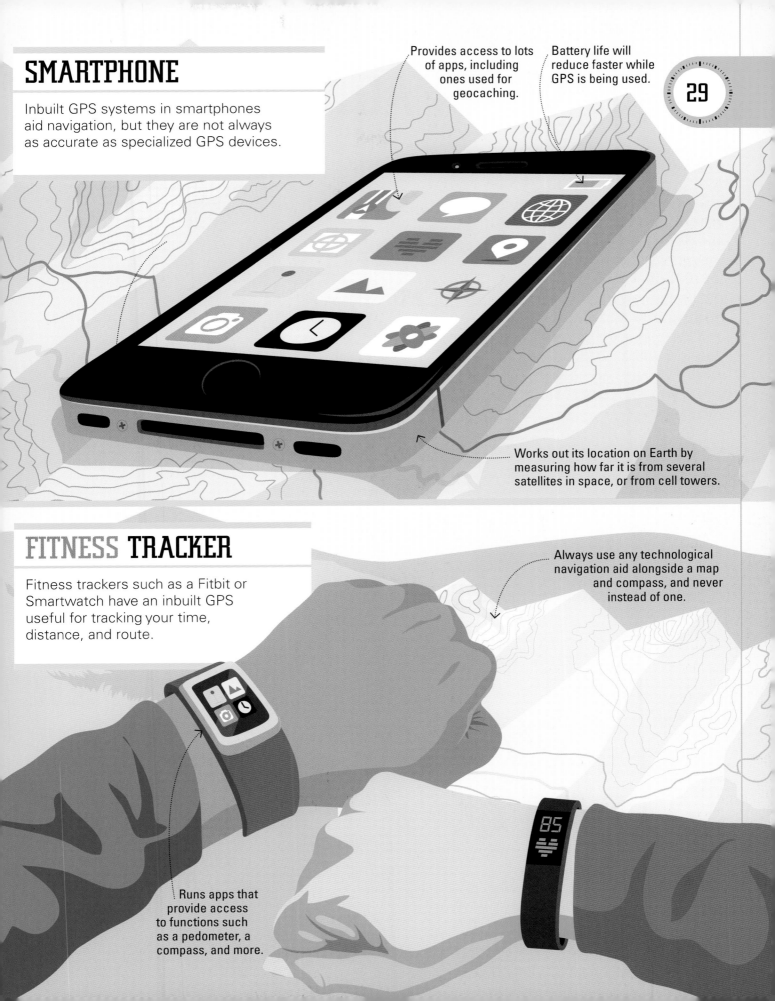

SMARTPHONE

Inbuilt GPS systems in smartphones aid navigation, but they are not always as accurate as specialized GPS devices.

Provides access to lots of apps, including ones used for geocaching.

Battery life will reduce faster while GPS is being used.

Works out its location on Earth by measuring how far it is from several satellites in space, or from cell towers.

FITNESS TRACKER

Fitness trackers such as a Fitbit or Smartwatch have an inbuilt GPS useful for tracking your time, distance, and route.

Always use any technological navigation aid alongside a map and compass, and never instead of one.

Runs apps that provide access to functions such as a pedometer, a compass, and more.

Even the best-planned hikes can run into difficulties, so it is essential that others know **where you are and what you are doing**. An action plan provides important information for potential rescuers, so that they have the **best chance of finding you** and your group – and looking after you when they do. Always tell someone where you are going and when you expect to return.

CREATE A PLAN ON A PHONE APP TO ALERT FAMILY AND FRIENDS.

Sketch your route, or photocopy or photograph a map. Add timings for points along the way.

Supply contact details for you and your family. Include your full name and any nickname.

Name:

Age:

Email:

Route and timings:

Lakeview carpark
Ⓟ

Lakeview Drive

Pine Road

Depart 10am
Return 4pm
Lunch 1-2pm

Crystal La...

STEP BY STEP

❶ Provide the names, ages, height, and weight of all members of your group. List mobile phone numbers and detail any communication devices, such as radios.

❷ Give details of health issues, injuries, or allergies among your group. Write down the medication that anyone is taking or carrying. Note any first aid supplies.

❸ Detail your kit – and level of experience – so rescuers can try to understand how you will cope with certain weather conditions or an unexpected night out.

WHISTLE AND TORCH

Keep a whistle on a cord round your neck. Use this, or a light, to make the International Emergency Signal.

1 Blow six short blasts on your whistle.

2 You can do the same with a light (flash it six times) if you have a torch.

3 Wait, repeat, and listen for the reply: three signals.

REFLECTED SIGNAL

Placing a torch on a reflective silver survival blanket will make the light more noticeable.

1 Find a wide, open space to spread the blanket.

2 Peg out the blanket or use stones to weight its corners.

3 Place your light, set to flashing mode, in the centre.

CATHERINE WHEEL

Create a bright "Catherine wheel" with a chemical glow stick. This can be seen 3 km (2 miles) or more away.

1 Tie the glow stick to a cord about 1 m (3 ft) long. Use shoelaces if necessary.

2 Activate the glow stick by bending then shaking it.

3 Whirl it in front of you to create a circle of light.

BUILD A SIGNAL FIRE

Imagine you are lost and **you need to call for help**, but your phone is out of battery, or your backpack, with your emergency equipment inside, has been washed away. Don't panic. **A fire is an effective way of signalling** – clouds of white smoke are visible by day, and flames can be seen at night. A signal fire requires materials and hard work.

FOR WHITE SMOKE, USE GREEN VEGETATION. AT NIGHT, USE DRY WOOD FOR FLAMES AND LIGHT.

FIRE - SEE PAGES 94-97

The inside of the dome burns to produce smoke. The dome also shelters the fire to stop it going out.

Build your fire on flat ground in the open, so it can be seen easily.

Use tent pegs or strong, hooked sticks to peg poles into place.

STEP BY STEP

❶ Lay two long poles parallel to each other. Prop up the ends on rocks or logs, and peg the ends down. Use four forked stakes to support the poles.

❷ Lay green wood sticks in between the forked stakes to form a platform. The upright ends of the stakes will hold the platform in place.

❸ Bend two long saplings to criss-cross over the platform. To secure the saplings firmly in place, dig their ends into the ground, like tent pegs.

Green foliage, fur boughs, and leaves create lots of white smoke.

SIGNAL MIRROR

Polish the end of a drink can with charcoal and water, toothpaste, or even chocolate. Hold the polished base up to face the sun. Do not look directly at the sun, which can damage your eyes. Reflect light onto your hand, then move your hand up and down to flash signals. A mirror, the shiny surface of a survival tin, or the inside of a crisp packet can be used instead of a drink can.

Keep a supply of dry, green vegetation nearby to feed the fire.

The raised fire allows airflow, making it easier to light and to draw in oxygen.

Never leave the fire unattended, stay away from smoke, and don't get too close to the fire.

❻ Use your lighter, or flint and steel, to light the fire. If you think rescuers are coming, wait until you hear them before starting the fire. Remember, it can take a couple of minutes for smoke to be generated.

❹ On the platform, lay materials for a large fire – tinder, kindling, and fuel (see pages 96–97). Top it off with green vegetation. Don't light the fire just yet.

❺ Add several layers of green vegetation to form a domed roof. Leave a small opening so that you can access the fire to light it and maintain it.

CHAPTER 2

ON THE TRAIL

UNDERSTANDING THE DANGERS POSED BY AN ENVIRONMENT, ITS CLIMATIC CONDITIONS, BOTH DAY AND NIGHT, AND BY THE ANIMALS THAT LIVE IN IT WILL HELP YOU PLAN A SAFE TRIP.

The great outdoors
Across the globe, trails across an incredible range of landscapes give walkers the opportunity to explore the natural world.

WEATHER RISKS

A weather change can add danger to a trip, affecting temperature, visibility, the state of the ground, and morale. Weather on top of a peak can be different to that at the bottom, so prepare for both.

Heavy rain
In heavy rain, the ground may become slippery. Seek shelter or put on waterproofs and proceed with caution.

Fog
A cloud at ground level, fog reduces visibility. If you can't see where you're going, stop walking and take shelter.

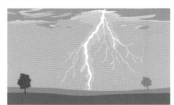

Lightning
A lightning bolt will strike the first object it meets, so avoid high, exposed places and never shelter under a tree.

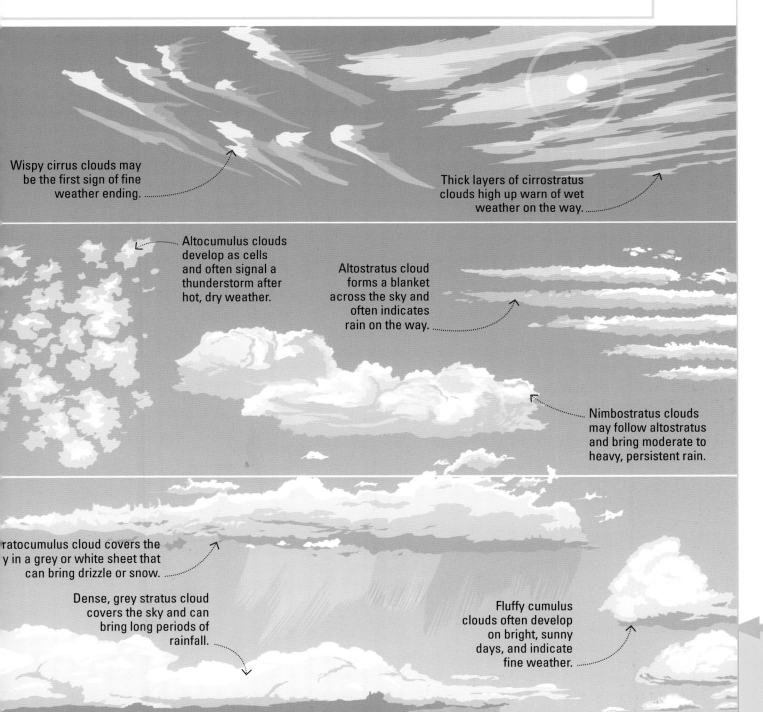

Wispy cirrus clouds may be the first sign of fine weather ending.

Thick layers of cirrostratus clouds high up warn of wet weather on the way.

Altocumulus clouds develop as cells and often signal a thunderstorm after hot, dry weather.

Altostratus cloud forms a blanket across the sky and often indicates rain on the way.

Nimbostratus clouds may follow altostratus and bring moderate to heavy, persistent rain.

ratocumulus cloud covers the y in a grey or white sheet that can bring drizzle or snow.

Dense, grey stratus cloud covers the sky and can bring long periods of rainfall.

Fluffy cumulus clouds often develop on bright, sunny days, and indicate fine weather.

Biting, stinging **creepy-crawlies** are found in all parts of the world. Before you set out on a trip, **familiarize yourself** with the harmful insects and arachnids (spiders, scorpions, and ticks) in the region you are visiting. **Venomous** effects range from an itchy, painful nuisance to life-threatening poisons. **Bites and stings** may trigger allergic reactions, and some species are carriers of serious diseases. Here are some to look out for.

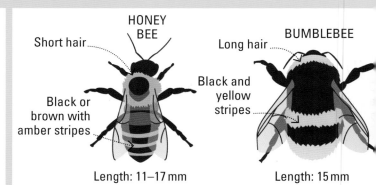

HONEY BEE — Short hair — Black or brown with amber stripes — Length: 11–17 mm

BUMBLEBEE — Long hair — Black and yellow stripes — Length: 15 mm

Bee species live worldwide, building nests in trees and holes in the ground. Look out for bees feeding in flowers and take care not to disturb nests. A bee stings only once, but can cause severe allergic reactions in some people.

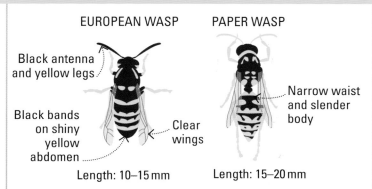

EUROPEAN WASP — Black antenna and yellow legs — Black bands on shiny yellow abdomen — Clear wings — Length: 10–15 mm

PAPER WASP — Narrow waist and slender body — Length: 15–20 mm

European wasps make nests underground and in logs, while paper wasps nest in branches. Take care if gathering fruit or cleaning fish as the smell will attract wasps, which can sting repeatedly.

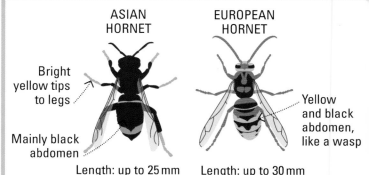

ASIAN HORNET — Bright yellow tips to legs — Mainly black abdomen — Length: up to 25 mm

EUROPEAN HORNET — Yellow and black abdomen, like a wasp — Length: up to 30 mm

About twice the size of wasps, hornets can bite and sting, but are less aggressive, stinging only when provoked. They make nests in hollow tree trunks or hanging from branches.

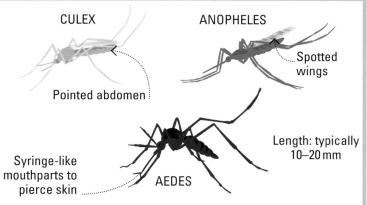

CULEX — Pointed abdomen

ANOPHELES — Spotted wings — Length: typically 10–20 mm

Syringe-like mouthparts to pierce skin — AEDES

Mosquitoes live near water in warm regions. The bites of females can irritate the skin and some carry diseases such as malaria. Cover skin at dusk, use repellent, and sleep under a net.

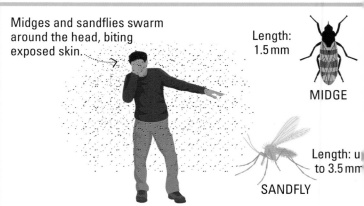

Midges and sandflies swarm around the head, biting exposed skin.

Length: 1.5 mm — MIDGE

Length: up to 3.5 mm — SANDFLY

Tiny, bloodsucking flies found near water, biting midges and sandflies can be a nuisance in summer, passing through nets and getting into tents. Cover skin with light clothing and apply repellent.

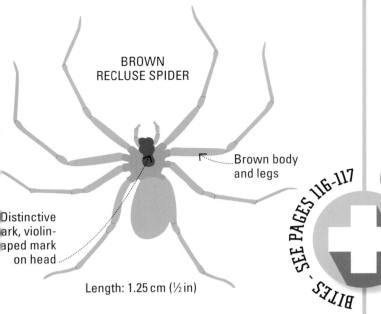

BROWN RECLUSE SPIDER

Brown body and legs

Distinctive dark, violin-shaped mark on head

Length: 1.25 cm (½ in)

Found in the southern US Midwest, this spider is known as a fiddleback. Its bite is rarely fatal, but can cause fever, chills, vomiting, and joint pain. It hides in dark places, so always check boots and bedding.

BITES – SEE PAGES 116–117

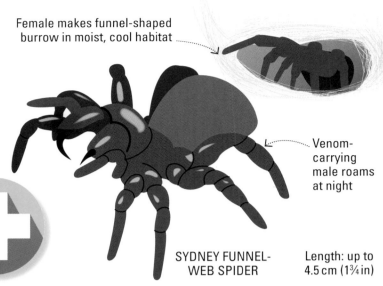

Female makes funnel-shaped burrow in moist, cool habitat

Venom-carrying male roams at night

SYDNEY FUNNEL-WEB SPIDER

Length: up to 4.5 cm (1¾ in)

The venomous Sydney funnel-web spider has a glossy black body and short legs. Its painful bite causes sweating, nausea, and weakness, but is rarely fatal. Take care when moving rocks and logs.

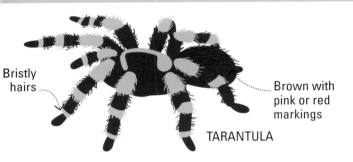

Bristly hairs

Brown with pink or red markings

TARANTULA

Length: up to 14 cm (5½ in); leg span: up to 28 cm (11 in)

Tarantulas are giant spiders that live in tropical forests. They hunt at night and have a mildly venomous bite. If irritated, tarantulas flick itchy hairs from their abdomen. Move away if you see one – don't touch it.

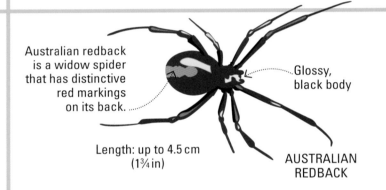

Australian redback is a widow spider that has distinctive red markings on its back.

Glossy, black body

Length: up to 4.5 cm (1¾ in)

AUSTRALIAN REDBACK

Small, dark widow spiders live in warm regions worldwide. Their painful bite can lead to sweating, chest pains, and nausea. It is rarely fatal. Watch out for webs in shrubs or among rocks or logs.

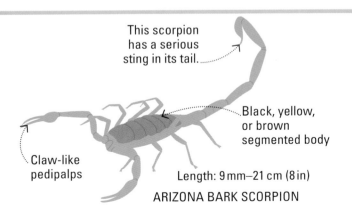

This scorpion has a serious sting in its tail.

Black, yellow, or brown segmented body

Claw-like pedipalps

Length: 9 mm–21 cm (8 in)

ARIZONA BARK SCORPION

Scorpions live in warm regions worldwide. Their very painful stings may cause severe illness and temporary paralysis, but are rarely fatal. Check boots and beds, and take care when gathering firewood.

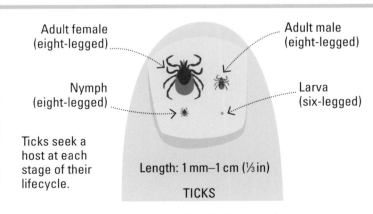

Adult female (eight-legged)

Adult male (eight-legged)

Nymph (eight-legged)

Larva (six-legged)

Ticks seek a host at each stage of their lifecycle.

Length: 1 mm–1 cm (⅓ in)

TICKS

Found in woods and grassland, ticks feed on warm-blooded animals (hosts). They can carry disease. Wear long trousers and use a repellent. Check skin and brush off ticks before they dig in.

ANIMAL ENCOUNTERS

When outdoors, you might meet **wild animals**. Most try to avoid contact with humans, but some, especially bears, might come closer looking for food. If animals are **provoked**, cornered, or surprised, they may attack to defend themselves, especially if they have young.

BEARS

When walking in bear country, equip yourself with bear spray and bells (see the panel on page 47).

If a bear stands up, it is trying to work out what you are; it is not the first step of an attack.

HEY!

Never turn your back on a bear; face it and observe it all the time.

❸ If the bear approaches you, make noise and wave your arms. If it comes closer, and looks about to attack, stand your ground. Use your bear spray or throw objects.

STEP BY STEP

❶ If you come across a bear and it spots you, stay calm, talk to the bear, but avoid eye contact. Ready your bear spray.

❷ Make yourself as large as possible and group close together if you are with others. If the bear keeps its distance, back away slowly. Do not run or climb a tree.

❹ In case it does attack, if it's a black bear, fight for your life, aiming to hit its eyes and nose. If it's a brown bear, drop face down and play dead.

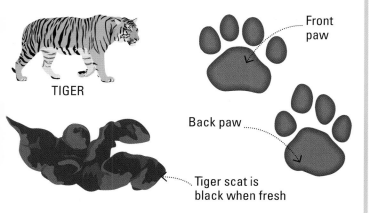

TIGER

Front paw

Back paw

Tiger scat is black when fresh

Tigers live across Asia, with Bengal and Siberian tigers being the largest in size. Like other big cats, they prefer a carnivorous diet and their scat is full of hair, sometimes from much larger animals.

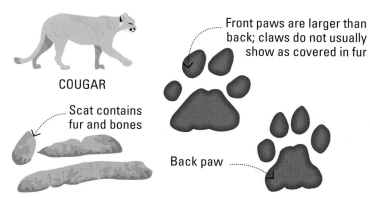

COUGAR

Front paws are larger than back; claws do not usually show as covered in fur

Scat contains fur and bones

Back paw

Cougars, also known as mountain lions or pumas, are the largest cat in the Americas. They are shy, but encounters are becoming more common as people hike and camp in their habitats.

BLACK BEAR

Front paw

Bear scat from spring diet, rich in meat

Back paw

Black bears live in mountainous areas across North America and encounters are common in nature reserves. Omnivores, they can run fast, swim, and climb. An average male weighs over 130 kg (287 lb).

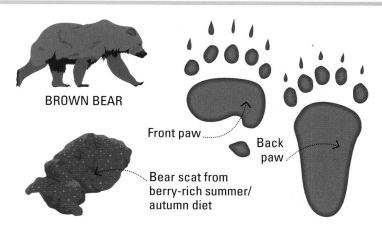

BROWN BEAR

Front paw

Back paw

Bear scat from berry-rich summer/autumn diet

Brown bears inhabit the wilds of northern Eurasia and North America. Also omnivorous, they are larger and heavier than black bears. Their toes are closer together and less curved, with longer claws.

WOLF

Front paws are larger

Back paw

Tapered droppings containing fur

Wolves roam in packs across habitats in northern North America and Eurasia. Humans are not natural prey, but wolves can attack if they feel threatened. Tracks are bigger than those of dogs and coyotes.

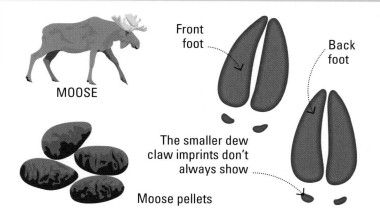

MOOSE

Front foot

Back foot

The smaller dew claw imprints don't always show

Moose pellets

Moose are common in Canada, northern USA, Scandinavia, the Baltic states, and northern Russia. The largest of the deer family, they leave oval pellets, up to 3 cm (over 1 in) long.

Heat exhaustion can develop when the body heats up and cannot **cool down**. If not recognized and treated, it can quickly develop into **heatstroke**, which must be treated as an **emergency**. **Prevention** is better than a **cure**, so follow these tips to avoiding a **heat injury**.

WARNING!

Call emergency services for help if these signs of heat exhaustion develop and become worse:

- headache
- pale, clammy skin
- dizziness and confusion
- fast breathing or pulse
- cramps
- loss of appetite
- excessive sweating
- feeling sick

Neck flap protects neck from burning.

Loose clothing helps to keep you cool.

Keep your water bottle handy – many backpacks have pockets for bottles.

❶ If possible, avoid walking when the day is at its hottest. Walk in the shade, wear a hat and sunglasses, and apply sunscreen often.

MAKE YOUR OWN SHADE

STEP BY STEP

❷ Drink frequently, even if you don't think you are thirsty, so that your body stays hydrated. The body loses water through sweat and this needs to be replaced.

Place layers in backpack

❸ Layers allow you to add and remove clothing in order to regulate your body heat. Take off layers if you are too hot to help your body cool down.

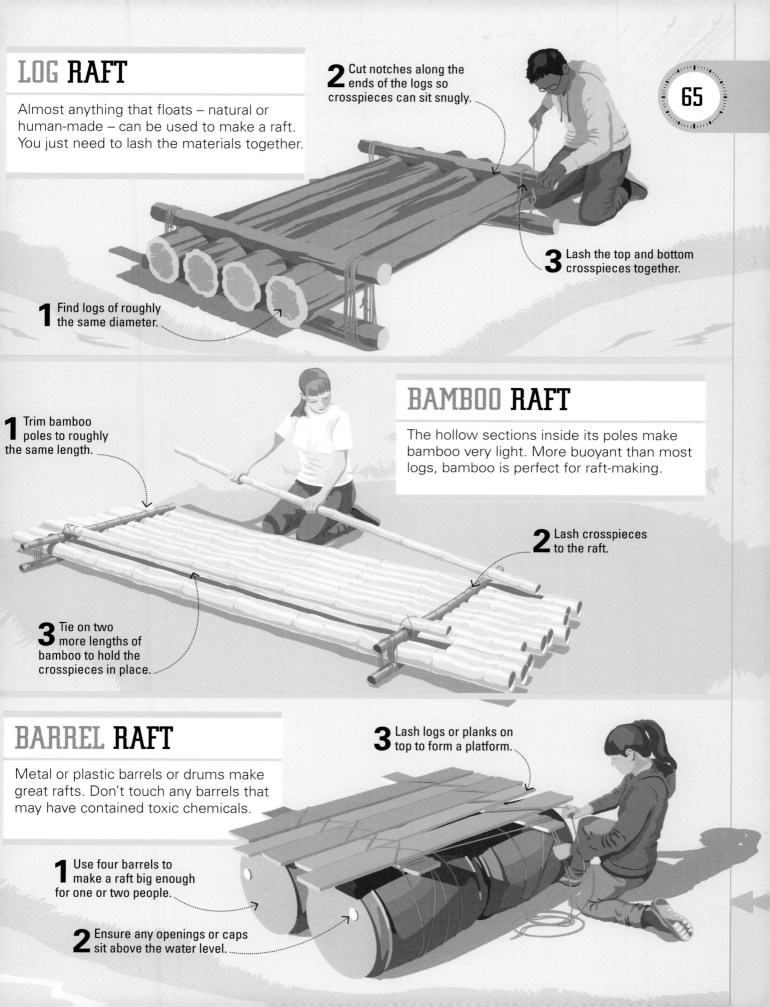

LOG **RAFT**

Almost anything that floats – natural or human-made – can be used to make a raft. You just need to lash the materials together.

2 Cut notches along the ends of the logs so crosspieces can sit snugly.

3 Lash the top and bottom crosspieces together.

1 Find logs of roughly the same diameter.

BAMBOO **RAFT**

The hollow sections inside its poles make bamboo very light. More buoyant than most logs, bamboo is perfect for raft-making.

1 Trim bamboo poles to roughly the same length.

2 Lash crosspieces to the raft.

3 Tie on two more lengths of bamboo to hold the crosspieces in place.

BARREL **RAFT**

Metal or plastic barrels or drums make great rafts. Don't touch any barrels that may have contained toxic chemicals.

3 Lash logs or planks on top to form a platform.

1 Use four barrels to make a raft big enough for one or two people.

2 Ensure any openings or caps sit above the water level.

CANOE RESCUE

In a canoe, the paddler kneels or sits and uses a single-bladed paddle on one side. Keep a canoe stable by **distributing weight evenly** and not overloading it. If you're with a group and you capsize, your best option is **canoe-over-canoe rescue**. This is a technique that uses a second canoe to help right the one that has overturned.

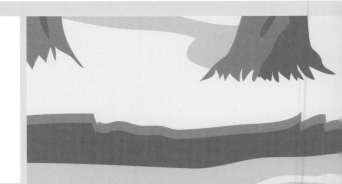

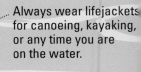

Crew of the rescue canoe help pull the capsized canoe up and across their boat.

Always wear lifejackets for canoeing, kayaking, or any time you are on the water.

Other people in the water should support the rescue canoe.

2 If you cannot turn the canoe, guide it towards a second, rescue canoe. Tip one end down to raise the other end up. The rescuers must pull the canoe up and slide it across their own boat, and rotate it to tip out the water.

Push down on this end of the canoe to lift up the other end.

STEP BY STEP

1 If you feel your canoe might overturn, head towards shallower water. If you do capsize, remain calm. Try to turn over the canoe in the water.

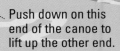

3 Rotate the canoe to its upright position and slide it into the water. The rescuer must hold both canoes together to allow you to climb aboard again.

Pack an emergency survival kit box containing: whistle, flares, locator beacon, first-aid kit, drinking water, and a reverse-osmosis pump or solar still (to make drinking water from seawater).

A recognition light helps rescuers spot the raft.

In the morning, soak up dew (fresh water) from the canopy with a cloth or sponge.

Collect rainwater in a bucket or bag. Catch water running off the canopy.

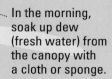

Solar still

Keep out of the sun, wind, and rain as much as possible. If the raft has no canopy, improvise one.

Droplets collect on the sheet and drip into the cup

❺ Place your still in a sunny position on the deck. As the seawater evaporates, it leaves the salt behind on the cloth. Freshwater droplets collect on the sheet and drip into the cup. The process is slow, but every drop means life.

❹ Secure the sheet to the top of the container with string. Make sure you can easily loosen it – you'll need to remove the sheet every few hours to re-soak the cloth.

WARNING! ⚠️

- Never drink seawater. It contains salt and will dehydrate you further.

- Dehydration is your number one enemy if you are adrift at sea (see page 101).

- Be aware that sea-sickness also leads to dehydration.

CHAPTER 3

CAMPCRAFT

WHETHER USING A TENT OR IMPROVISING A SURVIVAL SHELTER, IT IS ESSENTIAL THAT YOU KNOW HOW TO SELECT AND SET UP A CAMPSITE - A WELL-SELECTED SITE WILL HELP KEEP YOU SAFE.

Under the stars
At the end of a day of walking, nothing beats a hot meal and sitting by the warmth of the camp fire.

CHOOSING A CAMPING SPOT

When setting up your camp you should always take into account the **four principles of survival**: protection, location, water, and food. Make sure your **site is safe** and will protect you from the elements. Try to be close to a **water source**, materials needed for making a **shelter,** and fuel for a **fire**. In a rescue situation, choose a position where your location aids can be easily seen.

> **DON'T PICK A SITE USED BY WILD ANIMALS OR ONE PRONE TO FLOODING SHOULD IT RAIN.**

CAMPING TIMETABLE

Three hours before dark
Look around your chosen area for the most suitable site. Build your shelter and gather all the materials you will need to get a fire going and maintain it through the night. Collect water. Prepare location aids if in a rescue situation.

One hour before dark
Make sure all of your equipment is in one safe place so you can find it. If in a group, ensure that everyone knows where the emergency location aids are and how to use them. Use the toilet and wash. Avoid using a knife at night unless you have adequate light.

High ground has cold night-time temperatures, so is not a good camp location.

Sun-facing camp receives warmth and light

Woodland offers shelter and is a source of fuel.

Signal fire

Deadfall – watch out for falling dead branches

Sheltered location, entrance at right angles to wind

Have a supply of dry firewood that will last all night.

Ideally, build three signal fires, arranged in a triangle.

Location aids, once set up, require no more effort.

Running water a safe distance from camp reduces the risk of flooding and danger from animals and insects.

ASSESSING THE AREA

Before setting up camp, take some time to examine your surroundings and avoid any potential hazards.

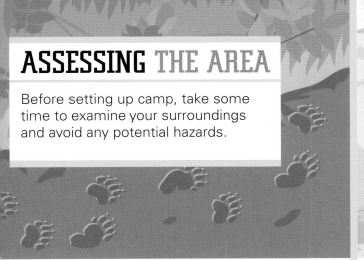

Look for signs of animals, especially near water, where they may come to drink. If spotted, pitch your shelter against a rock face so that it can only be approached from one direction.

Avoid areas inside river bends, which are prone to erosion and flooding during heavy rain, as well as river banks on outside bends, which may burst. In gullies there is a risk of flash floods.

Stagnant pools or standing water attracts swarms of insects, such as mosquitoes, which breed in them, so avoid camping next to these.

Rockfalls and icefalls can occur beneath mountain peaks, so check for cracks and fissures if camping near rocks. Heat rising from fires can cause rockfalls, and in the cold ice sheets can fall suddenly from rocks.

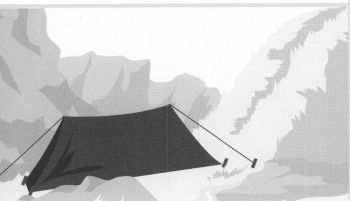

Sloping or poorly drained ground should be avoided as a camping spot. Also beware of rock slides and run-off from inclines during downpours.

Waterfalls and loud running water can be noisy enough to hide the sound of animals or rescuers, so camp away from these locations.

TENT BASICS

A shelter gives you **immediate protection** against the elements. Some modern tents can **weigh under 2 kg** (4⅖ lbs) and pack to the size of a tin of beans! Most modern tents use a **flexible pole system**, have **separate flysheets**, and are easy to erect when using instructions.

ALWAYS USE A WATER-PROOF GROUNDSHEET IN WET CONDITIONS.

PUTTING UP A TENT

Always practice putting up your tent before going camping, ideally both during the day and in the dark.

A taut flysheet allows rain to run off and not pool on the tent.

❸ Secure the flysheet over the inner tent, leaving a gap between them to prevent moisture on the flysheet from leaking inside. Peg the flysheet taut.

Loop the guyline around the peg and drive the peg into the ground. Adjust so the guylines are taut.

In dry, hot weather, you may not need the flysheet.

STEP BY STEP

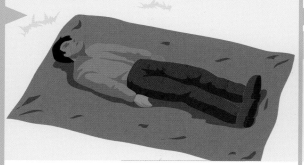

Position door away from wind

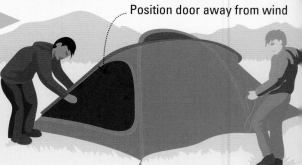

❶ Place your groundsheet flat on the ground and lie on it to check there are no stones or roots underneath. The groundsheet should not extend beyond the floor of the tent.

❷ Most tents have a pole and sleeve inner tent, and a separate flysheet. Erect the tent, position it over the groundsheet, and peg it into place using the loops around the edges.

MAKE A TENT PEG

Use wood from green trees when making tent pegs. Never use wood found on the ground – it could be rotten.

WARNING!

Never drive a peg into the ground with your foot. If you misjudge it, the peg may injure your ankle or foot. Use a stone or a heavy stick as a mallet instead.

1 Choose a piece of wood 22.5 cm (9 in) long and 2.5 cm (1 in) wide. Hold it steady, with the end you want to make into a point firmly on the ground.

2 Using your knife, shave off the wood in a downwards motion, pointing the sharp knife edge towards the ground. Slowly shave until you have a point at the end.

3 Cut a notch towards the top of the peg. This will help your tent's guylines stay securely around the peg.

Notch

Pointed end rests on the ground

KNIFE SAFETY – SEE PAGES 92–93

TIE A HANK

Keeping cordage – here paracord – in a hank stops it becoming a big ball of knots that you have to unpick later.

WARNING!

If you want to heat-seal the end of the paracord, do be careful if heat-sealing over a flame – when the paracord melts, it can drip and burn.

Stretch out your thumb and little finger to keep the cord from sagging.

2 Continue winding the cord in a figure of eight until you have about 20 cm (8 in) of cord left – this is the tail.

A hank of cordage can be 6–10 m (20–33 ft) long.

Tail

STEP BY STEP

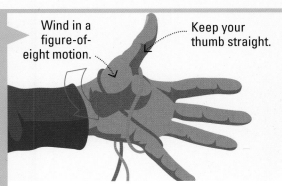

Wind in a figure-of-eight motion.

Keep your thumb straight.

1 Hold out your hand with your thumb and fingers spread out. Rest the end of the cord on your palm, then loop the cord in a figure of eight around your thumb and little finger.

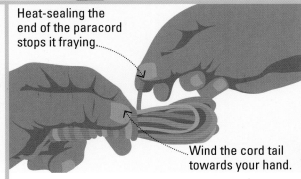

Heat-sealing the end of the paracord stops it fraying.

Wind the cord tail towards your hand.

3 Take the hanked cord off your thumb and little finger. Secure the hank by winding the tail tightly around it. Finish by tucking a loop under the last wind and pulling it tight.

In a **survival situation** you may need to spend a period of time **in one place** – maybe you **cannot move**, or staying where you are is the best option for **rescuers to find you**. Following some **simple rules** will help to ensure that when you set up a site, even for just one night, **you will remain safe** and won't put yourself or others in any more danger.

RESCUE TEAMS MAY BE IN THE AIR OR ON THE GROUND. LOCATE A SITE THAT BOTH CAN SEE.

FIRE AND FUMES

Fire safety around your camp is extremely important – out of control fires can be devastating and fatal.

Have a means of extinguishing your fire quickly – water, sand, or soil work.

Keep your fire a safe distance away from low, overhanging trees, and your shelter.

✓ Keep watch on your fire at all times.

✗ Don't leave the campsite until the embers are cold to touch.

✗ Don't position fire where smoke can pour into the tent.

✗ Do not have a naked flame (candles, cooking stoves, barbecues) inside your shelter/tent. This can result in a build-up of toxic carbon monoxide gas – which you can't see, hear, smell, or taste.

✗ Do not use accelerants (petrol, gas, methylated spirits) to start your fire – their vapour is invisible and can explode when ignited.

✓ Do keep the area around your fire clear and free from tripping hazards.

GOOD HOUSEKEEPING

A well organized site keeps you safer and ensures everyone knows where everything is stowed.

BUILD A FIRE - SEE PAGES 96-97

✓ Designate areas for tools, emergency signalling devices, and other important items – so everyone knows where they are and can get to them easily and safely.

✓ Pack away items not in immediate use – they are less likely to get lost.

✓ Keep important equipment inside your shelter, where it will keep dry.

✗ Do not set up toilet facilities too close to your camp, but DO make sure the loo is easy to locate in the dark (see pages 90–91).

✗ Do not leave possessions out in the open after dark – they'll get wet if it rains or dew falls in the night.

✗ Do not cut firewood once it gets dark – even cutting firewood by torchlight can be dangerous.

KEEP OUT!

Whilst you should have picked a site safe from wild animals, you should still do all you can to not encourage a visit.

ANIMAL ENCOUNTERS - SEE PAGES 44-49

Bears, rats, mice, and other creatures may trespass into your campsite on their hunt for food.

DO'S

✓ Keep food away from your site, off the ground, and in animal-proof containers.

✓ Hang up your boots on a post and keep clothes packed away to keep out insects.

✓ Check for stinging or biting insects by shaking out clothes and sleeping bags, and by tapping out boots before putting them on.

✓ Always keep the tent zipped up to prevent animals entering.

DON'TS

✗ Don't reach into concealed spaces, backpacks, sleeping bags, or boots, without checking – small animals, spiders, or snakes may have crawled in!

✗ Don't leave dirty cooking or eating utensils around after eating – they attract scavengers, so clean immediately.

✗ Don't prepare or cook food close to your tent, as it can attract animals.

✗ Don't leave your torch on if not needed – the light attracts unwanted insects.

Before you set off on a trip, learn the best **knots** for **particular tasks**, such as attaching a line to a tree, and **practise** tying them. Skill with knots is not only useful but saves wasting cordage. Usually, a correctly tied knot **unties easily**, so you can **re-use the same cordage** many times.

The ends of the line

The end doing the least work is called the standing end.

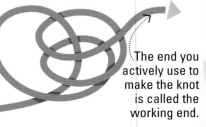

The end you actively use to make the knot is called the working end.

Half hitch

A single half hitch knot is unsafe when used alone but holds firmly when doubled or trebled. It is often used to make another knot more secure.

Put the line through the fixture, loop the working end over the line.

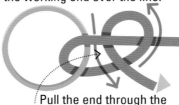

❶ Pull the end through the middle of the loop just made.

For a double half hitch, again loop the end over the line and pull through the middle of the new loop.

❷

Reef knot

The reef knot (or square knot) is good for securing a line around an object or joining two lines together. Do not use it for jobs that need a secure knot, as it can work itself apart.

❶ Form a bight with the end of the standing line

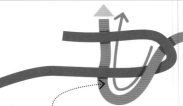

❷ Pass the end of the working line through the bight and around both parts of the standing line.

Fisherman's knot

This easy and reliable knot is used for tying hooks to single-fibre (monofilament) fishing line. It does not work well with a multi-stranded (braided) line.

❶ Pass the line through the eye of the hook.

Loop the working end over the line, winding it round 5–6 times.

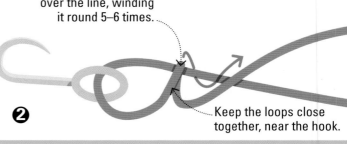

❷ Keep the loops close together, near the hook.

Arbor knot

Use this all-purpose knot to tie the end of a line to a fixed point or to lash things together.

Then pass the working end through the loop you have just made.

❶ Pass the line around the fixture and loop the end around the line.

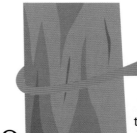

❷ Repeat step one, on only the working end of the line, close to the first knot.

Slip knot

A slip knot is a great example of a simple knot that has many practical uses. One end tightens and one end loosens. Pull both ends to undo completely.

Form an underhand loop

❶

Make a loop with the working end and pass it through the first loop.

Second loop

First loop

❷

Hold this loop

Hold the tip of the loop you just passed through and pull the standing end tight.

❸

Clove hitch

This handy knot is simple to tie and untie. A clove hitch can slip if not under constant pressure, so combine it with two half hitches for more security.

First, place the line around the fixture.

Then loop one end around the fixture again.

❶

Pass the end underneath the line sitting on top.

❷

Pull both the ends outwards to tighten.

❸

❸

Pass the end of the working line back through the bight.

Pull both parts of each line to tighten the knot.

❹

Pass the working end through the loop next to the eye.

Pass the working end down through the loop you have just made.

❸

Pull end down

Pull until the knot cinches tightly onto the eye of the hook.

❹

❸

Pull the standing end to cinch both knots together.

Pull the working end to loosen the knot.

❹

Pull the standing end to tighten the knot.

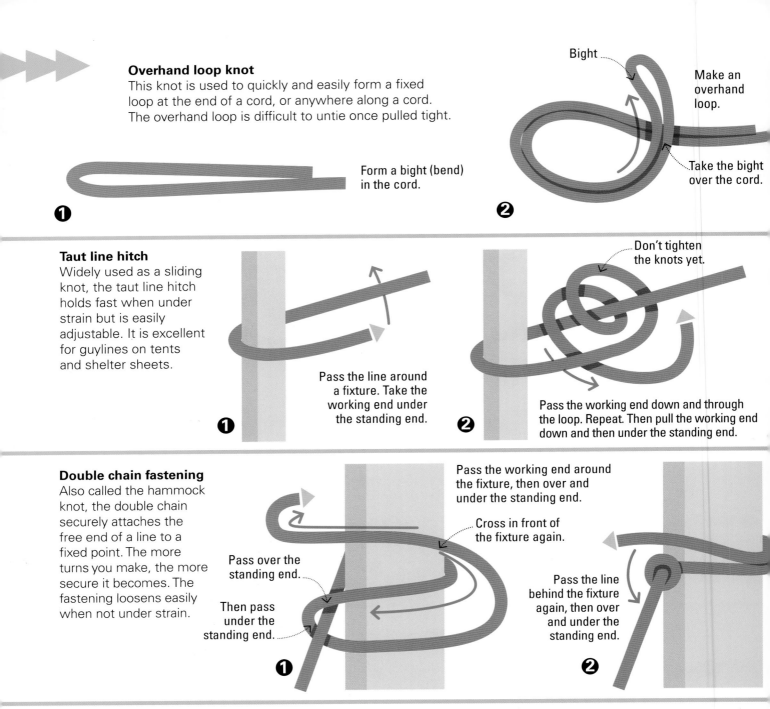

Overhand loop knot
This knot is used to quickly and easily form a fixed loop at the end of a cord, or anywhere along a cord. The overhand loop is difficult to untie once pulled tight.

Form a bight (bend) in the cord.

❶

Bight

Make an overhand loop.

Take the bight over the cord.

❷

Taut line hitch
Widely used as a sliding knot, the taut line hitch holds fast when under strain but is easily adjustable. It is excellent for guylines on tents and shelter sheets.

Pass the line around a fixture. Take the working end under the standing end.

❶

Don't tighten the knots yet.

Pass the working end down and through the loop. Repeat. Then pull the working end down and then under the standing end.

❷

Double chain fastening
Also called the hammock knot, the double chain securely attaches the free end of a line to a fixed point. The more turns you make, the more secure it becomes. The fastening loosens easily when not under strain.

Pass the working end around the fixture, then over and under the standing end.

Cross in front of the fixture again.

Pass over the standing end.

Then pass under the standing end.

❶

Pass the line behind the fixture again, then over and under the standing end.

❷

Siberian hitch knot
Also known as the Evenk knot, this is good for quickly attaching a line to a fixed object, such as a ridgeline for a shelter.

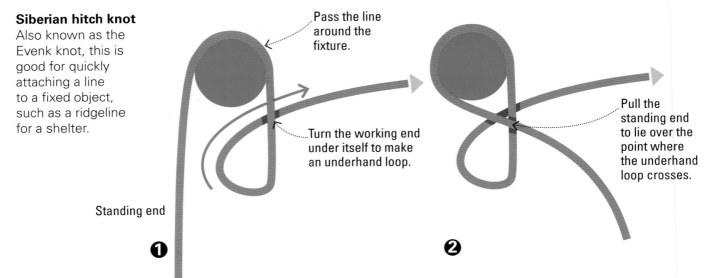

Pass the line around the fixture.

Turn the working end under itself to make an underhand loop.

Standing end

❶

Pull the standing end to lie over the point where the underhand loop crosses.

❷

TREE SHELTERS

Constructing other shelters is great fun. Remember the aim is to stay safe, warm, and dry. Use the methods learned in the building of the A-frame shelter to make tree shelters from broken, uprooted, and fallen trees.

Broken trunk
Tie off a ridgepole to a tree instead of using an A-frame at the front.

Uprooted tree
Build a roof over the higher roots and hollow at the base of an uprooted tree.

Fallen tree trunk
Use the side of the tree trunk to build a roof – like one side of the A-frame shelter below.

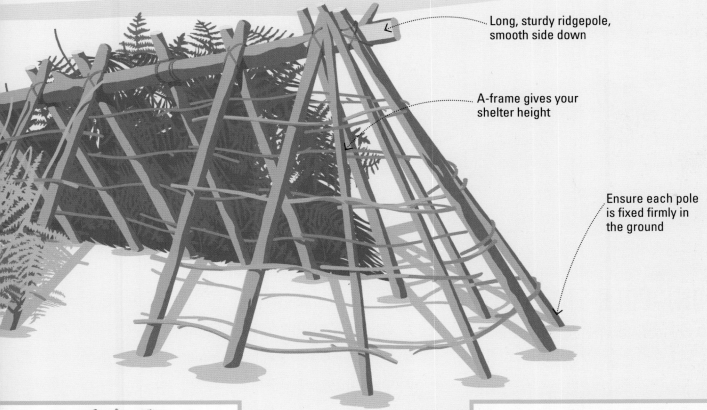

Long, sturdy ridgepole, smooth side down

A-frame gives your shelter height

Ensure each pole is fixed firmly in the ground

3 Weave rows of saplings horizontally through the poles to form a latticework, leaving a gap for your entrance. Ensure the entrance is large enough for you to get in.

4 Cover the latticework frame using whatever natural materials are available. Pine boughs or anything with a large leaf, such as ferns, work well.

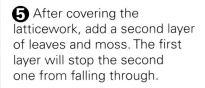

5 After covering the latticework, add a second layer of leaves and moss. The first layer will stop the second one from falling through.

In a survival situation you need **immediate protection** from the elements as being cold and wet can quickly and seriously affect your ability to function. Packing a **space blanket, tarp, shelter sheet, or poncho** means you have the ability to quickly make a simple shelter and get out of bad weather.

KNOTS - SEE PAGES 80-83

Pile vegetation such as leaves around the base of shelter to keep out wind.

Siberian hitch knot

Angle pegs at 40 degrees from shelter.

You can use your backpack to form a partial door.

ONE-POLE SHELTER

A one-pole shelter uses cordage and a stick to make a basic shelter from the wind and rain.

❹ Find a long stick about 1 m (3 ft) for a centre pole and place it inside the middle of the shelter to give height and keep the sides taut. Cushion the spot (by using a spare sock, for example) where the pole meets the sheet so it doesn't tear through.

STEP BY STEP

60 cm (2 ft) 2 m (6 ft)

60 cm (2 ft) 60 cm (2 ft)

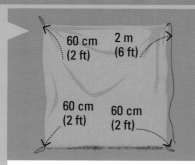

Peg out so tarp is taut

❶ Cut 3 x 60-cm (2-ft) cords. Pass each one through a corner and make a loop with a reef knot. Cut a 2-m (6-ft) cord and tie to the last corner with a Siberian hitch knot.

❷ Tie the long cord on the fourth corner to a tree at a height of 1 m (3 ft) off the ground with another Siberian hitch knot.

❸ Making sure the opening to the shelter faces away from the wind, peg out the other three corners.

OTHER SHELTERS

While the one-pole shelter is the easiest to improvise, there are other quick shelters that you can make. Practise building these shelters, so that it becomes second nature. If you have a little more room in your backpack, carry a bothy bag – a basic emergency shelter that is ready to use and will protect you from the elements.

A-frame
Tie cord between two trees with a double-chain knot. Drape over a tarp to create an A-frame. Attach cord loops (see Step 1, opposite) to peg it out.

Hooped shelter
Form three hoops from saplings or softwood trees and peg out the corners of your tarp or poncho over them.

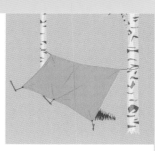

One-sided shelter
Attach one side of a tarp to a line between two trees and peg the other end to the ground at an angle. This will form a basic wind break.

MAKE A BUTTON TIE

If your shelter material has no loop or grommet to which to attach a line, make a button tie. This makes a secure fastening without cutting holes in the material, keeping it waterproof and less likely to rip.

Stone inside the material

❷ Place the open loop of the slip knot over the neck of the button and pull it tight.

STEP BY STEP

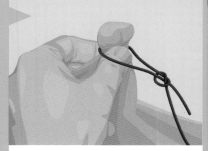

❶ Wrap a small, round, smooth stone in the material to form a "button". Prepare a length of cord with an open loop of a slip knot at one end.

❸ At the other end of the cord, make a simple overhand loop to place over your shelter pegs.

Personal hygiene when outdoors is very important. Keeping yourself clean helps to **keep you healthy** by reducing the risk of infection, sores, and illness. It is also important to a positive **state of mind** – when hygiene slips, often everything else follows!

Grip a tree to help you balance.

POO IN THE WILD

In a survival situation, or just out in the woods, you may get caught short. Here is the right way to poo outdoors.

❷ Remove your trousers and pants or have one leg out. If in a skirt, keep it gathered above your hips. Squat over the hole, and hold the tree for support while you take care of business.

Always carry travel tissues and hand sanitizer.

STEP BY STEP

❶ In a private spot, clear a 1-ft- (30-cm-) square area an arm's length from a tree. Use a stick to dig a hole, piling soil beside it. Put toilet paper and sanitizer nearby.

❸ With the business done, you can now stand up. Before doing anything else, wash your hands using sanitizer or water. You can now sort your clothing.

❹ With your stick, use the pile of soil to entirely cover the toilet hole. Place two crossed sticks on top of the area, so others know that this spot has been used.

MAKESHIFT SHOWER

You can buy camping showers, but if you have an empty container or spare bucket you can make one easily.

Low tree branch

If water pours out too fast, put leaves or stones in the bottom to slow it down.

4 Hook the shower over a bowed sapling or a low branch. Fill with water warmed over a fire or left to warm in the sun. Be careful not to let the water become too hot.

STEP BY STEP

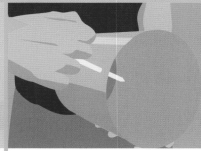

1 Turn the container upside down on a flat surface. Then carefully punch holes in the bottom with the point of your knife or a nail.

2 Make a hole about 2.5 cm (1 in) down from the rim of the container. On the other side make a matching hole. Use a rock to smooth out any rough edges.

3 Thread cord more than 60 cm (2 ft) long through the holes so about 30 cm (1 ft) is on either side. Tie the ends with an overhand knot (see pages 82–83).

DAILY HYGIENE

Check for ticks and insects. Avoid fungal infections by washing every day. Your hair will regulate itself.

Rinse eyes with water twice a day.

Check head for insects and bites.

Rub teeth and gums with a clean finger.

Wash hands, feet, crotch, and armpits.

A **pocketknife** and a **small saw** can be the most useful items to have in your **survival kit**. Knowing how to **use a knife and saw safely** will reduce the likelihood of injuring yourself or others. A pocketknife has many uses, from **cutting cordage and twigs** to **preparing food**.

DON'T USE A KNIFE UNTIL YOU HAVE BEEN SAFELY TAUGHT HOW.

KNIFE SAFETY

● When using a knife make sure everyone around you is aware you have an open knife. Keep a clear and safe working circle (shown below), making sure there are no hazards within your arm's length.

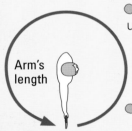

Arm's length

● Always keep your knife closed unless you are actually using it. Use a solid base to support your work – such as the ground. Never use a part of your body, such as your thigh, to support your work.
● Always cut away from yourself.

OPEN AND CLOSE A KNIFE

OPEN Hold the knife in one hand, with your thumb along one side and your other fingers along the opposite side. Use the thumb and index finger of the other hand to open the blade away from you until it clicks into place.

CLOSE Hold the knife in the same way as when you opened it. Pinch the back of the blade with your thumb and index finger, then slowly fold the blade fully back into the body of the knife.

WARNING!

In the UK, it is illegal to:

● Sell a knife to anyone under the age of 18, unless it has a folding blade that is 7.62 cm (3 in) long or less.

● Carry a knife in public without good reason, unless it has a folding blade with a cutting edge that is 7.62 cm (3 in) long or less.

● Carry, buy, or sell any type of banned knife.

● Use any knife in a threatening way (even a legal knife).

● Carry a knife or tool with a blade that locks.

KNIFE CARE

✓ Ask an adult to always keep your blade sharp as a sharp knife is safer than a blunt one.

✓ Clean your knife after use and make sure it is dry before storing away.

✓ Lightly oil the blade and any moving joints.

✓ Keep your knife in a sheath or pouch on your belt.

WOOD SAW BASICS

- Always make sure the wood you are to saw is securely held against a solid surface, such as a flat rock or log.

- Use your foot or hand to keep the wood steady whilst you saw.

- Make sure you wear shoes for protection when using your foot to hold the wood in place.

- Keep your hands a safe distance from the saw blade, as it might slip.

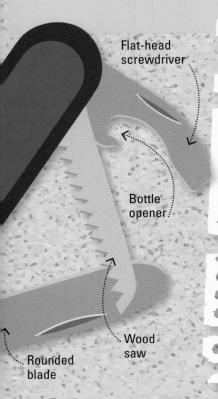

Flat-head screwdriver

Bottle opener

Wood saw

Rounded blade

HOLD A KNIFE

Always hold the knife with a firm but relaxed grip. Positioning your grip close to where the handle joins the blade reduces strain on the wrist.

DO'S

- Always close your knife before handing it to someone else.

- When using a knife always have a first aid kit at hand.

- Always cut away from yourself and others.

- Wearing gloves can give an extra layer of protection.

- Do all of your cutting in daylight, when you can see what you are doing safely.

HOW TO CUT WITH A SAW

Using the wood saw blade is a safer way to cut wood and it uses less energy than cutting with a small knife. Saw blades are extremely sharp, so always keep your fingers away from the teeth. Cut on a solid surface and make a starting groove before applying pressure. You can use your foot to help secure the piece being cut, but wear protective footwear.

DON'TS

- Don't throw your knife – it is extremely dangerous and can also damage your knife.

- Never stick your knife in the ground when not using it – always put it back in its sheath.

- Don't use a knife with cold or wet hands, or when tired.

- Don't thow your knife at a tree – it can bounce straight back at you!

- Don't use a knife in the dark, or under torchlight or candlelight.

The **three material elements** you need to build a fire are **tinder, kindling, and fuel**. They must be dry and plentiful. A well-made **feather stick** effectively provides all three elements on one piece of wood. It can be lit easily with a match or lighter or even from a **spark**, with practice. Making them is good fun.

The "feathers" act as tinder. Other sources of tinder include birch bark, dry grass, and fine wood shavings.

KNIFE SAFETY – SEE PAGES 92–93

The thin part of the stick is kindling. Small, dry dead pieces of wood, as thin as a match or as thick as your finger, are used to get the fire going.

The end you are holding is the fuel. Dry, dead fuel creates a bed hot coals that sustain your fire with lit effort. Additional fuel logs should be about as thick as your forearm.

❸ Turn the stick and run the knife down the edge to create a second shaving, then keep working around it until you have a thin stick with curled shavings attached.

STEP BY STEP

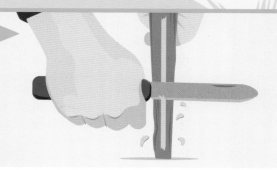

❶ Choose a straight, dry stick with no knots. Lay your blade flat on the stick and run it all the way down the stick, trying not to cut into the wood at first. This helps you feel how your blade moves over it.

❷ Tilt the angle of the blade towards the wood and run it down to cut a shaving, stopping just before the bottom so that the shaving stays attached to the stick. Don't worry if at first you cut the shaving off.

MAKING SPARKS

Lighting your tinder is the first step to making a fire. **Matches** or a **lighter** do this easily, but being able to light tinder using a **spark** is a great skill! A **flint and steel** – a ferrocerium or magnesium alloy **rod** combined with a steel **striker** – is waterproof and produces thousands of sparks.

Blowing gently on the flames adds oxygen.

THE COMPONENTS OF FIRE

OXYGEN — HEAT — FUEL

Place your ball of tinder on a fire platform.

! For fire safety, see page 78

Use your boot to hold the hand that is holding your striker steady.

❹ Keep making sparks until the tinder has caught fire – ensure you remove your hands and feet away from the flames immediately. Make sure you have lots of kindling and fuel ready to add – at least twice what you think.

STEP BY STEP

❶ Gather your tinder, kindling, and fuel (or feather stick, opposite). Place a ball of tinder on your fire platform and place the end of the rod in the centre of the tinder.

❷ Place your striker onto the rod and lock the hand holding the striker in position. Resting your hand on your boot helps.

Scrape the rod up the striker

❸ Pull the rod up and away from the tinder, drawing it against the striker to make sparks. Drawing it up avoids disrupting your tinder.

The importance of being able to **make and maintain a fire** cannot be understated. Fire can keep us **warm, dry, and safe from wild animals**. Fire can also be used to **boil water**, so it's safe to drink, and to **cook food**. We can use fire to **signal** for help, too. Things never seem so bad when you are sitting in front of a fire.

CARRY TWO METHODS OF LIGHTING A FIRE – AND KNOW HOW TO USE THEM.

WARNING!

- Check local fire restrictions and don't build a campfire at a site with dry conditions.
- Make your campfire in a designated area only, and keep your campfire small and under control (for fire safety see page 78).
- Always keep water nearby to put out fire.

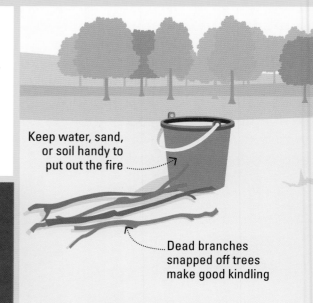

Keep water, sand, or soil handy to put out the fire

Dead branches snapped off trees make good kindling

ELEMENTS OF FIRE – SEE PAGES 94–95

Do rake dry twigs and leaves well away from the fire using feet or a branch, not your hands

STEP BY STEP

Kindling

Tinder

Fuel

❶ Gather the materials you need to light your fire: tinder, kindling, and fuel (see pages 94–95). You'll need more than you think, so multiply everything by ten!

Platform protects the ground

Wood or rocks help contain the fire

❷ Choose the place for your fire and clear the ground of dry leaves and twigs. Lay a platform of green wood. Use four larger bits of wood to contain the fire.

Start with small pieces of kindling

Tepee of kindling

❸ Place the tinder on the platform and make sparks to light it (see page 95). Let the flame catch. Gently lay kindling on the flame so it looks like a tepee.

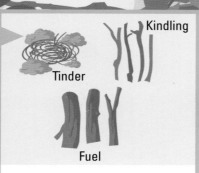

Keep fire away from overhanging tree branches and leaves

Do not position the fire where wind will blow smoke into your shelter

Control your fire and make sure you don't set fire to anything you don't mean to, such as exposed tree roots

Regularly add pieces of fuel to keep the fire burning.

5 Continue to add two pieces of fuel at a time to create a "log cabin" effect. The fire is established when it can be left for five minutes without going out. Remember to never leave a fire unattended.

Do not build your fire close to old logs and fallen trees

4 As the kindling catches fire and the flames grow, add larger pieces of kindling, gradually building up to larger fuel logs. Fanning the flames with a map gives the fire extra oxygen.

6 Before you leave the campsite, douse your fire thoroughly with water. Make sure all the embers are out.

Hotter, drier summers around the world in recent years have increased the **risk of wildfires**. When vegetation on the ground is **tinder dry**, the slightest **spark** can start a fire that quickly sweeps through a forest.

ALWAYS PUT OUT CAMPFIRES—ONE SPARK CAN START A WILDFIRE.

❸ The direction of the smoke tells you which way the wind is blowing. Wind chases fire, so getting up-wind of a wildfire is safer. Fire is drawn faster uphill, so don't go up.

STEP BY STEP

❶ If venturing into a forest, check local radio reports for fire risk and carry a mobile phone. Let others know your route and have an evacuation plan.

❷ Stay alert to signs of fire. You'll smell a fire first, hear it crackling, and see clouds of smoke, or ash falling from the sky, before seeing it. Don't panic but don't hang around.

DO'S AND DON'TS

Humans cause more than 80 per cent of forest fires. Campfires are a common cause – never leave them unattended. See pages 78–79 on camp safety.

✓ Check local fire restrictions and don't build a campfire at a site where conditions are dry.

✓ Make your campfire in a designated area only.

✓ Keep your campfire small and under control.

✓ Allow your campfire to burn completely to ash. To extinguish it, douse it with water to drown all embers. Keep pouring water on it until the hissing sound stops and make sure everything is cold to the touch before you leave.

✓ Never leave a fire unattended.

If the wind is blowing towards the fire, move quickly into the wind.

WIND DIRECTION

See pages 62–63 about crossing water safely.

Remember to leave a space to breathe.

Dampen clothing and cover yourself with dirt.

④ If the wind is behind the fire, it will move very fast. A wildfire needs fuel, so look for an area without fuel such as a river, clearing, or road.

⑤ If you can't escape, get as low as possible. Dig a trench in damp soil and lie face down with your feet facing the flames. Hold your breath as the fire goes over you.

THE IMPORTANCE OF WATER

Water is essential to life. It is needed for **every physical and chemical process** that takes place in your body. You need a **steady supply** of water to sustain yourself in a survival situation, and **without it you will dehydrate**.

ALWAYS CARRY A WATER BOTTLE THAT CAN PURIFY WATER.

Brain
Water makes up approximately 80 per cent of the brain.

Nose, mouth, and eyes
Water keeps soft tissues such as the mouth, nose, and eyes moist.

Blood
Water makes up 83 per cent of blood and plays an important role in regulating blood pressure.

Lungs
Water helps to moisten the lungs and assists breathing.

Stomach
Water helps the body to digest food in the stomach and turn it into energy.

Liver and kidneys
Water reduces pressure on the liver and kidneys as it flushes out waste products.

Intestines
Water aids digestion and dissolves minerals and other nutrients to make them accessible to the body.

Bladder
Water enables the bladder to flush out waste through urine.

Bones
Water makes up approximately 22 per cent of bones.

Muscle
Water makes up 23 per cent of muscles.

Skin
Water keeps the skin moist. The evaporation of sweat (water) from the skin also regulates body temperature.

Joints
Water provides cushioning for joints.

MAKE A TRAIL MIX

A good trail mix can help you **replace the energy and nutrients** you use when outdoors. You can purchase ready-made trail mix, but it's also easy and great fun to **make your own**. Once made, you can **store** your trail mix in an **airtight container**. Before your next outing, **scoop portions into ziplock bags** so everyone in your group has their own supply to snack on.

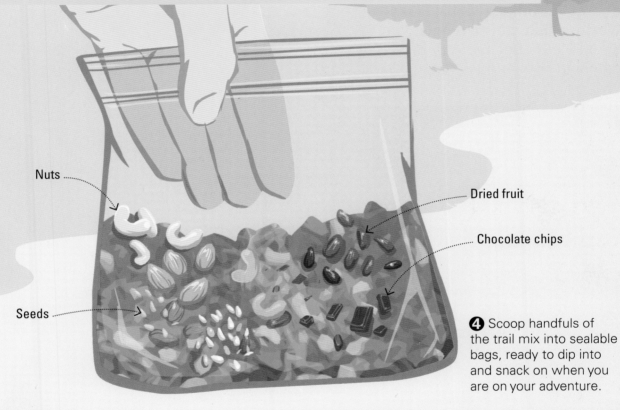

Nuts

Seeds

Dried fruit

Chocolate chips

❹ Scoop handfuls of the trail mix into sealable bags, ready to dip into and snack on when you are on your adventure.

STEP BY STEP

❶ Making your own trail mix is quick and easy. First wash your hands. Then gather your favourite trail mix ingredients, such as edible nuts, seeds, dried fruit, chocolate, and cereal.

❷ Take a large bowl or container. Measure equal quantities of nuts such as cashew nuts, almonds, and brazil nuts and add them to the bowl. Add sunflower seeds and pumpkin seeds.

❸ Add chocolate chips, dried fruit such as raisins and cranberries, and dried cereal for sweetness. You can also add popcorn. Mix it all together.

NET A FISH

Fish are **high in protein** so are a great food source. Once you have made a **trap**, or **baited and set a fishing line**, it works for you 24/7 with no additional effort, which means you have extra energy for other survival tasks. **Netting fish** can also be a simple and effective way of catching fish – and is fun!

COOK A FISH - SEE PAGES 110-111

FISH LIKE DEEP, STILL WATER, ESPECIALLY IN SHADOWY BENDS.

A dipping net will catch small fish at the edges of streams and lakes, particularly where trees cast shadows over the water.

Take care near banks of water – they can be slippery.

4 Place the net into the water where you see fish. Let the fish swim over or into the net. Be patient.

STEP BY STEP

1 Cut two small nicks in a T-shirt's hem and push the forks of a branch through them. If no hem, cut evenly spaced holes and push the branch in and out of them.

2 Cut another nick in the side of the hem where the forks meet, pull them through, and bind them together with string or rope.

3 Tie off the T-shirt above the armholes and neck. Cut off excess material, or invert the net, to reduce the size and prevent extra drag when netting.

MAKE A BOTTLE TRAP

A **bottle trap**, also known as a "minnow trap", is an easy way to **catch small fish**. The **inward-facing funnel opening** of the trap allows the **fish to get in**, but the small size of the opening means **they can't get back out again**. Lots of small fish can make a meal or be used as bait for bigger fish.

ONCE MADE AND BAITED, THIS TRAP WILL WORK FOR YOU ON ITS OWN, 24 HOURS A DAY.

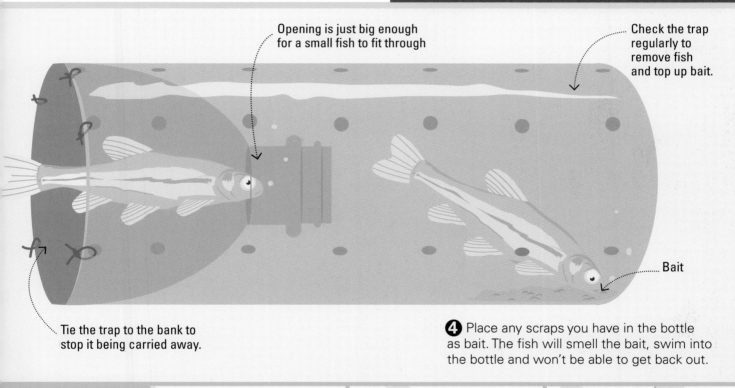

Opening is just big enough for a small fish to fit through

Check the trap regularly to remove fish and top up bait.

Tie the trap to the bank to stop it being carried away.

Bait

❹ Place any scraps you have in the bottle as bait. The fish will smell the bait, swim into the bottle and won't be able to get back out.

STEP BY STEP

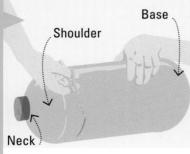

Shoulder

Base

Neck

❶ Using scissors or a knife, carefully cut off the top of a large, plastic bottle where the shoulder starts to narrow, making two pieces – a bottle neck and a base.

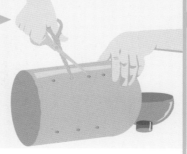

❷ Using the points of your scissors, carefully make lots of small holes in the bottle base so it will fill with water and sink. Make some holes near the open edge, too.

❸ Make two holes on the neck, near the edge. Insert the neck into the base as above, lining up the holes with those on the base. Tie the two pieces together.

USING LINES AND BAIT

Fishing **equipment** can be made from all sorts of material. Your survival kit should have some fishing line and a few hooks, but if you don't have a kit you can improvise. You can use a stick as a **makeshift rod**, for example. Passive methods such as **night lines** mean that you can sleep, or do other tasks, while they work for you.

Use overhand loop knots (see pages 82–83) to make the loops.

With hooks placed at even intervals, you can attract fish that live at different depths.

NIGHT LINE

With hooks, a fishing line, and a rock, you can easily make a simple fishing device that will do the work for you.

Keep hook leader lines short to avoid them getting tangled.

STEP BY STEP

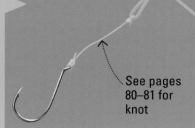

See pages 80–81 for knot

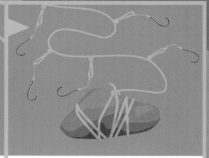

❶ Make loops along the fishing line. Attach shorter leaders to each loop, and a hook to the other end. Use fisherman's knots for both.

❷ After attaching all the hooks, making sure they are spaced evenly along the line, tie a rock to one end of the line to weigh it down.

❸ Tie the line to a post stuck securely in the ground at the bank's edge. Add the baits. Throw the line into the water and leave overnight.

IMPROVISED HOOKS

Fishing hooks can be crafted from any piece of metal, such as a nail, needle, wire, or safety pin.

3 Tie a second, smaller nail to form a barb.

2 Angle the nail away from the wood and lash into position.

1 Cut a notch into a piece of wood and place the head of a small nail in it.

NAIL HOOK

2 Bend the back of a safety pin at an angle to form a barb, as shown.

1 Remove the safety clasp so that the bare, bent end makes a hook.

METAL PIN HOOK

FLOATS

You can make a float from any natural material that floats – a piece of bark, a berry, or a rose hip, as shown here.

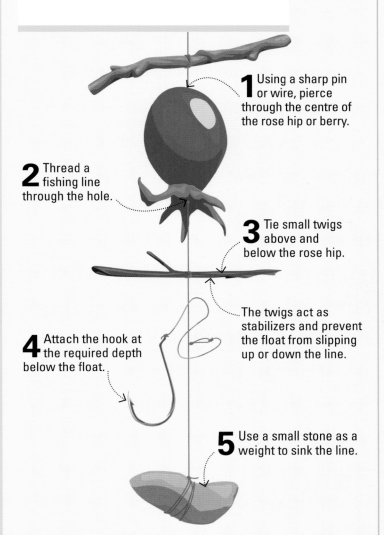

1 Using a sharp pin or wire, pierce through the centre of the rose hip or berry.

2 Thread a fishing line through the hole.

3 Tie small twigs above and below the rose hip.

The twigs act as stabilizers and prevent the float from slipping up or down the line.

4 Attach the hook at the required depth below the float.

5 Use a small stone as a weight to sink the line.

TYPES OF BAIT

Worms
Worms attached to a hook attract some fish. Caterpillars, slugs, or maggots also work.

Insects
Insects such as crickets (above) and beetles are natural prey for many fish.

Small fish
Some big fish eat smaller fish – catch small fry in a bottle trap like the one on page 107.

Nuts and fruit
Tie small nuts, bits of bigger nuts, and small pieces of fresh or dried fruit to the hook, or pierce them.

Food scraps
Bread, cheese, and pasta can work. Some fish will eat animal meat and guts.

COOK A FISH

Fish are easier to prepare and cook than most animals, so should be a **first choice** for food if they are available. Fish **must be cooked** to **kill any parasites and bacteria.** Never eat a fish that does not look healthy – you can use it as bait instead.

TO KILL A FISH, CLUB IT JUST ABOVE THE EYES WITH A HARD OBJECT.

DO'S AND DONT'S

Here are some key things to remember when preparing food outdoors. It is important to keep things cleans to avoid getting sick.

✓ Food cooking can attract wild animals and insects, so cook away and downwind of your shelter site.

✓ Ensure your hands are cleaned before and after preparing and eating.

✓ Clean your pocketknife blade using alcohol wipes from your first aid kit before using it on any food

✓ Take no chances, overcook rather than undercook any food.

✓ Eat food straight after cooking it, and ideally downwind of your shelter site.

✓ In a survival situation there are no such things as leftover scraps of food. Eat everything – it is fuel your body needs.

✓ Wash all cooking pots and utensils in hot water if you have it, otherwise wash in running water to remove residue that could develop infectious germs.

KNIFE SAFETY – SEE PAGES 92-93

STEP BY STEP

❶ Hold the fish by its tail and scrape off the scales, holding the knife blade away from you and moving towards the head.

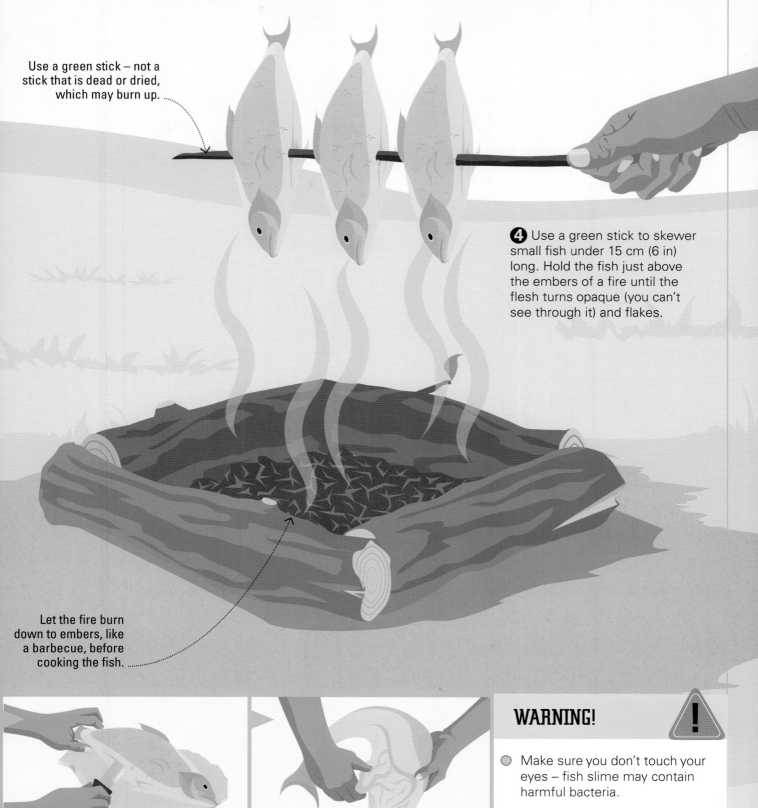

Use a green stick – not a stick that is dead or dried, which may burn up.

4 Use a green stick to skewer small fish under 15 cm (6 in) long. Hold the fish just above the embers of a fire until the flesh turns opaque (you can't see through it) and flakes.

Let the fire burn down to embers, like a barbecue, before cooking the fish.

2 Hold the fish, belly towards you. Holding the knife blade away from you again, insert the knife point into the anal orifice and slit open from belly to throat.

3 Pull out all of the internal organs and wash the fish thoroughly inside and out. Keep the organs to use as bait.

WARNING! ⚠

- Make sure you don't touch your eyes – fish slime may contain harmful bacteria.

- Always wash your hands before and after handling fish.

- Use a stick from a tree you can identify. Some sticks are harmful to use as a skewer for cooking.

CHAPTER 4

FIRST AID

A BASIC UNDERSTANDING OF FIRST AID IS ESSENTIAL IN THE WILD. MOST MEDICAL PROBLEMS, SUCH AS DEHYDRATION, CAN BE AVOIDED BY RECOGNIZING EARLY SYMPTOMS AND PREVENTING THEM DEVELOPING.

Essential kit
You can buy a ready-made first aid kit, or put together your own. If you can, go on a first aid course to learn and understand more skills.

FIRST AID KIT

Safety is key on any expedition. Before you set off make sure you have an understanding of **basic first aid** and all the **necessary medications and equipment** you might need. Check the seals on sterile dressings; if they're not intact, they're not sterile. **Replace any kit as soon as you use it**.

KEEP YOUR FIRST AID KIT DRY AND READILY ACCESSIBLE.

Tick extractor tool
Use to remove ticks safely.

Triangular bandages
Use to make slings.

Plasters
Take fabric, waterproof, hypoallergenic, and blister plasters.

Pain relief medication
Take medicine such as ibuprofen or paracetamol to relieve pain. Always follow the instructions on the packet.

Tweezers
Useful for removing splinters.

Aloe vera
Use on burns to reduce inflammation.

Latex-free disposable gloves
Wear gloves when treating animal bites.

Medical tape
Use to secure gauze or sterile dressings when covering cuts, grazes, or burns.

Scissors
Useful for cutting dressings or bandages to size.

Safety pins
Use to secure bandages.

Antihistamine tablets
Use to treat allergic reactions and itchy insect bites. Always follow the instructions on the packet.

Sterile dressings
It's helpful to have pads and dressings in assorted sizes.

Gauze roller bandages
Use to make support dressings, for example, for a sprained ankle.

Antiseptic cream
Use on minor cuts to prevent infection.

Anti-diarrhoea medicine
Use to treat sudden diarrhoea and prevent dehydration. Always follow the instructions on the packet.

Antiseptic gel or wipes
Clean your hands before touching cuts and grazes to prevent infection.

MAKE A SLING

If you trip over, you tend to use your hands to break the fall. This can result in a **broken wrist, forearm, upper arm, or collarbone**. If this happens, you need to **support the injury** by using a **sling** until you can get medical help. If the arm cannot be bent, it may be a broken elbow – in which case, **wrap padding around the joint** and **secure the arm to the body**.

ALMOST ANY PIECE OF CLOTH CAN BE USED TO MAKE SLINGS.

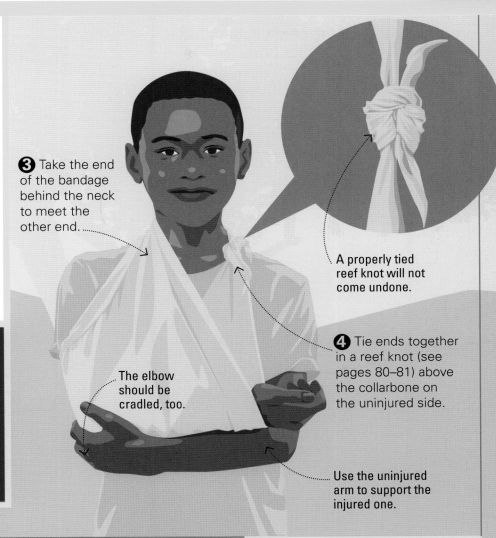

❸ Take the end of the bandage behind the neck to meet the other end.

A properly tied reef knot will not come undone.

The elbow should be cradled, too.

❹ Tie ends together in a reef knot (see pages 80–81) above the collarbone on the uninjured side.

Use the uninjured arm to support the injured one.

STEP BY STEP

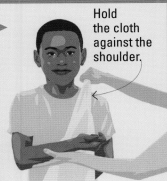

Hold the cloth against the shoulder.

❶ Fold a cloth, ideally about 1 sq m (11 sq ft), into a triangle. While supporting the injury, slip one end of the cloth under the injured arm, and the other end over the opposite shoulder.

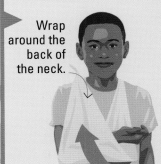

Wrap around the back of the neck.

❷ Fold the end that's hanging down up and over the injured arm, making sure it covers the elbow, too.

COLLAR AND CUFF SLING

The smaller loop supports the injured arm.

Use a belt or tie to make a simple collar and cuff sling. Fasten the item to form a loop. Place it over the head, then twist it once to form a smaller loop at the front. Place the injured arm through the smaller loop.

Vomiting and diarrhoea can be serious because they cause your body to lose **essential fluid**, leading to **dehydration**. If you feel nauseous, or experience vomiting or diarrhoea, you should rest, keep warm, and replace lost fluids.

WARNING!

- If you have a fever, severe belly pain, or prolonged (more than 24 hours) vomiting or diarrhoea, or if you see blood in your vomit or diarrhoea, seek urgent medical attention.

- When using medicines, always follow the instructions on the packet.

2 Drink clear fluid, starting with small sips, gradually drinking more.

3 Find somewhere safe to sit or lie down and rest until you feel better.

1 To control vomiting, avoid solid food. Then eat bland, light food such as crackers.

CAUSES OF SICKNESS

Heat exhaustion
Being in the sun for long periods of time can cause heat exhaustion and nausea (see page 52). Always wear a hat when you are out in the sun, drink plenty of water, take regular breaks, and seek shade if you feel yourself overheating.

Dehydration
Not drinking enough water can cause you to feel unwell and dehydrate (see pages 100–101). You must replace lost fluid from sweating, vomiting, or diarrhoea by drinking water in small sips rather than big gulps.

Stomach bug
Coming into contact with bacteria in the wilderness can cause sickness and diarrhoea. To prevent the spread of bacteria, wash your hands with soap and water before you eat and after you go to the toilet, or use a hand sanitizer.

Food poisoning
When food is not cooked or stored properly it can become contaminated with bacteria (see page 111). You may feel the effects within a few hours and you will often be sick or have diarrhoea. Lie down and rest, and drink plenty of water in small sips to prevent dehydration. If you feel hungry, eat plain food such as crackers, rice, bread, or pasta.

BURNS AND BLISTERS

There is a serious **risk of infection** with all scalds and burns. They may only affect the outermost layer of skin, the upper layers, or the full thickness. If a scald or burn is **larger than your hand**, then it needs **hospital treatment**.

1 Cool the injury for at least 10 minutes by dousing it with cool water. This will reduce pain and swelling.

STEP BY STEP

2 Protect the injury to reduce the risk of infection. Cover the entire area with a clean, sterile, non-fluffy material or dressing. Cover the burn loosely and take care not to burst any blisters.

TREATING BLISTERS

A blister is a fluid-filled "bubble" of skin that occurs when skin is burned or rubbed repeatedly against a surface (a friction burn).

Cover
To protect a blister from infection while it heals, cover it with a sterile dressing or blister plaster, or wrap gauze or a bandage loosely around the area. Never attempt to burst a blister yourself.

Fresh air
When you are not on your feet, remove the gauze or bandage to allow fresh air to reach the blister. This will help it to dry up and promote faster healing.

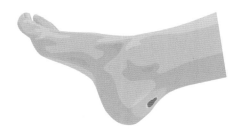

Reduce inflammation
Aloe vera has soothing, anti-inflammatory properties that make it excellent for treating blisters and reducing the redness and swelling that cause pain.

allergic reaction Sensitivity to a normally harmless substance, which causes the body's immune system to overreact. Symptoms commonly include a rash, sneezing, or swelling.

anaphylactic shock A highly dangerous allergic reaction to a substance such as insect-sting venom or a particular food.

antennae The pair of sensory organs, or feelers, on the heads of insects that are used to touch, smell, taste, and detect air movement.

bait Food placed on a fishing hook, or in a net or trap, to entice fish or other animals.

bearing The horizontal angle, measured in degrees, between an object and True North (north according to Earth's axis).

bight A loop of rope; also a curve in a geographical feature, such as a coastline.

bothy bag A large, waterproof bag used for protection or shelter.

cairn A human-made mound of stones built to mark a trail and be visible in fog.

canoe An open-deck paddle boat for one or more people.

capsized Of a boat, overturned in the water.

cardiac arrest Sudden stoppage of the heartbeat, which may be temporary or permanent.

carnivore An animal that eats other animals.

carrion The rotting flesh of dead animals.

cinch In a knot, to cinch means to "make certain" by pulling the knot tight.

climate The most common weather conditions in an area in general, or over a long period.

constellation A named group of stars that can be seen from Earth.

contamination The process of making something dirty, polluted, or poisonous by adding waste, chemicals, or infection.

contour lines Lines on a map that mark the changing height of the natural features of land.

compass An instrument used for orientation and navigation, using a freely rotating needle that indicates the direction of north.

cordage Lightweight rope.

current Strong movement of water in one direction.

dehydration A dangerous lack of water in the body caused by not drinking enough, or by sweating, vomiting, or diarrhoea.

detritus Discarded waste or debris; also material, such as rock fragments, caused by erosion.

disinfect To clean something to destroy any germs it may have.

downstream In the same direction that a river or stream is flowing.

dune A hill of sand on a beach or in a desert.

erosion Gradual wearing away of soil or rock by wind, water, or ice.

exertion Physical effort or exercise.

fatal Causing death by, for example, injury or illness.

fleece A soft, warm fabric used for clothing or as a lining material.

flysheet A waterproof sheet placed over a tent to add an extra layer of protection.

geocaching A treasure-hunting game played using GPS devices. Containers, called caches, are hidden in locations outdoors for players to try to find using GPS coordinates.

grid reference A number and letter used to pinpoint a specific location on a map.

hand sanitizer A liquid or gel that kills bacteria and germs.

hazard Something that could put you in a dangerous situation or cause an accident or illness.

heatstroke A serious medical condition caused by severe overheating.

hemisphere The northern or southern half of Earth divided by the equator, or the western or eastern half, divided by an imaginary line passing between the north and south poles.

hyperventilation Breathing much faster and deeper than normal. Symptoms include dizziness and feelings of panic.

hypothermia A life-threatening drop in body temperature.

infection A disease caused by bacteria, viruses, or parasites.

inflammation Painful redness and swelling caused by infection, burns, injury, or illness.

lashing A simple technique used to tie two things (for example, poles) together.

latticework Crossed-over strips of material, typically wood or metal, in a diagonal pattern.

lee side The side of something, such as a hill or tree, that is sheltered from the wind.

legend On a map, the key or information that explains symbols or colours.

lichen A tiny moss-like plant that grows on surfaces such as rocks, trees, and walls.

ligament A band of tissue that connects two bones together in a joint.

malaria A serious disease that is spread by mosquitoes in many tropical regions.

marsh An area of low-lying land that is often flooded and typically remains waterlogged at all times.

navigation The process of planning a route and finding a specific place using a map, compass, or GPS device. Natural features such as the Sun, Moon, and stars can also be used for navigating.

omnivore An animal that eats both plants and other animals.

orbit The circular path an object in space takes around another object when affected by its gravity.

paracord A slim, lightweight nylon rope, useful for lots of outdoor activities, for example, building a shelter.

paralysis The loss of muscle function and movement in a part of the body. It can be temporary or permanent.

parasite An organism that lives in or on another organism, known as the host, and often harms it.

Polaris The alternative name for the North Star, the star almost directly above Earth's north pole, which is often used for navigation.

prevailing wind A wind that blows predominantly from a single direction.

prey An animal that is hunted by another for food.

repellent A substance that deters insects or an animal from approaching closely.

satellite An object that is sent into space to orbit Earth to send and receive information.

scald An injury caused by very hot liquid or steam.

scat The droppings of any wild animal.

sterile Completely free of bacteria or any other microorgansim.

tarpaulin (tarp) A hard-wearing, waterproof sheet.

tendon A dense, fibrous cord of tissue that connects bone to muscle.

terrain The physical features of an area of land.

topography The features of an area of land, typically natural formations such as mountains, rivers, lakes, and valleys.

trail mix A mixture of dried fruit and nuts often eaten as a snack.

treading water Staying afloat in water in an upright position by moving the feet with a walking motion.

upstream In the opposite direction to which a river or stream is flowing.

vegetation Plants, particularly those found in a specific area.

venomous Describing an animal, such as a snake, that can inject venom (poison) through a bite or sting.

virus A disease-causing microbe that infects the cells of living things.

ACKNOWLEDGMENTS

DK would like to thank the following for their assistance with this book:
Joanna Penning for the index.

Picture credits
The publisher would like to thank the following for their kind permission to reproduce their photographs:
(Key: a-above; b-below/bottom; c-centre; f-far; l-left; r-right; t-top)

2-3 Alamy Stock Photo: Carrie Cole.
4 Alamy Stock Photo: Frode Koppang (tr); MITO images GmbH (cr). **5 Alamy Stock Photo:** NPS Photo (tl); Stas Tolstnev (clb); Kittisak Srithorn (c). **6 Alamy Stock Photo:** Frode Koppang. **12-13 Alamy Stock Photo:** MITO images GmbH. **38-39 Alamy Stock Photo:** NPS Photo. **72-73 Alamy Stock Photo:** Stas Tolstnev. **112-113 Alamy Stock Photo:** Kittisak Srithorn. **122-123 Getty Images:** Richard Hutchings.

All other images © Dorling Kindersley
For further information see:
www.dkimages.com

BEAR ENCOUNTER

Never turn your back on a bear. Stay calm and if it approaches, make a noise. If a black bear attacks, fight. If a brown bear attacks, play dead.

AVOIDING SNAKES

To deter snakes, tap the ground with a stick. If encountered, keep still and it should slip away. If the snake attacks hit hard on the head.

SHARK ATTACK

If you see a shark, try to swim calmly to safety. If it rushes at you, face it head-on and strike the tip of its snout, or gouge at its eyes and gills.

ESCAPE QUICKSAND

If trapped in quicksand, lie on your back with limbs outstreched, and paddle with your hands to solid ground.

UP OR DOWN?

To find which way is up if buried in an avalanche dribble saliva – it will flow down, so you can dig up and out towards the surface.

FIND SOUTH BY THE STARS

In the southern hemisphere, locate the four main stars of the Southern Cross constellation. Find its two pointer stars, imagine a line between them, and trace a line at right angles to meet a line through the Southern Cross. At the point the two lines meet, drop a line to the horizon to find south.